ROUND-UP 4

CONTENTS

1.	Present Simple – Present Continuous	3
2.	Past Simple – Present Perfect	9
3.	Adjectives – Adverbs – Comparisons	17
4.	Will – Be Going To	25
	Revision Exercises I	33
5.	Present Perfect Continuous	37
6.	Past Continuous – Used To – Was Going To	42
7.	Reflective – Emphatic Pronouns / Both – Neither / Possessives	49
8.	Past Perfect – Past Perfect Continuous	56
	Revision Exercises II	63
9.	Functions of Modal Verbs	67
10.	Questtions – Question Words – Question Tags	77
11.	Infinitive (to + verb) – Gerund (verb + ing)	84
12.	The Passive	88
13.	Conditionals	96
	Revision Exercises III	103
14.	Relatives	107
15.	Reported Speech	113
16.	Prepositions of Place – Movement – Time	122
17.	Articles	128
18.	Wishes	132
	Revision Exercises IV	137
	Summary of Tenses	142
	Irregular Verbs	144
	Pre-Tests 1 – 4	145
	Wordlist	163

Introduction

Round-up Grammar Practice 4 combines games and fun with serious, systematic grammar practice. It is ideal for intermediate students of English.

Students see grammar points clearly presented in colourful boxes and tables. They practise grammar through lively, highly illustrated games and activities.

Round-up is especially designed for different students studying English in different ways.

It can be used:
- in class with a coursebook. Students do both oral work – in pairs and in groups – and written work in Round-up.
- after class. The 'write-in' activities are ideal for homework. Students can practise what they have learned in the classroom.
- in the holidays for revision, Round-up has clear instructions and simple grammar boxes, so students can study at home without a teacher.

The Round-up Teacher's Guide includes a full answer key and four progress tests plus answer keys.

Pearson Education Limited
Edinburgh Gate, Harlow
Essex CM20 2JE England

© Virginia Pagoulatou-Vlachou 1993
All rights reserved; no part of this publication may be reproduced, stored in a retrieval system, or transmitted in any form or by any means, electronic, mechanical, photocopying, recording or otherwise, without the prior written permission of the copyright holder.

First published in 1993 by E. Vlachou – "Express Publications".
First published by Longman Group Limited 1995.
This edition published by Pearson Education Limited 2000.

Printed in Spain
by Mateu Cromo

Illustrated by Chris Zmertis

ISBN 0582 344654

1. Present Simple – Present Continuous

Present Simple is used:	Present Continuous is used:
1. for **permanent** situations. She **works** in an office.	1. for **temporary** situations. He'**s staying** with some friends at the moment.
2. for **repeated** actions in the present, especially with adverbs of frequency. He often **buys** her flowers.	2. for actions happening at or around the **time of speaking**. He'**s looking** for a new job at the moment.
3. for **facts** which are permanently true. The sun **sets** in the west.	3. with **always** to express **annoyance** or **criticism**. He'**s always telling** lies!
4. for **timetables** or **programmes**. The lesson **starts** at 10 o'clock.	4. for **fixed arrangements** in the near future. I'**m flying** to London **tomorrow**. (It's all arranged. I've already bought the tickets. The time of the action is always stated or understood.)

Time expressions used with Present S.	Time expressions used with Present Cont.
usually, always, never, often, sometimes, every day/week/month/year etc.	now, at the moment, at present, always, tonight etc.

Adverbs of frequency (often, always, usually, sometimes etc.) are placed before main verbs but after auxiliary / modal verbs (be, have, can, will, must, shall etc.).
He **often goes** to the theatre.   He **is never** late.

1. Present Simple - Present Continuous

Non-Continuous verbs

Some verbs appear rarely in the continuous form. These verbs express a permanent state and they are: appear (= seem), be, believe, belong, cost, feel, forget, hate, have (= possess), know, like, love, mean, need, prefer, realise, remember, see, seem, smell, sound, suppose, taste, think, understand, want etc.

       I **understand** it now.   **NOT**   I am understanding it now.

1 Write the verbs in the third person singular.

1. I miss. He *misses*
2. I buy. She ....
3. I carry. He ....
4. I fix. He ....
5. I watch. She ....
6. I call. He ....
7. I go. He ....
8. I dry. She ....
9. I play. He ....

2 Put the verbs in the correct column in the 3rd person singular, then say them.

match, try, bake, dance, ring, keep, hit, work, teach, rise, hate, leave, smoke, arrive, smile, kiss, begin, cry, lose, dress, choose, rob, like, sleep

/s/	/ɪz/	/z/
after /f/, /k/, /p/, /t/	after /s/, /ʃ/, /tʃ/, /dʒ/, /z/	after other sounds
bakes	*matches*	*tries*

3 Choose a verb from the list and complete the text. You may use the negative.

make, get up, wake up, hurry, get, finish, do, let, shout, go, have, be

Maria always 1) *gets up* early in the morning. She 2) .... breakfast for her husband and children. Then she 3) .... the children ready for school. The children 4) .... usually .... easily and sometimes she 5) .... at them. They 6) .... to school with their father who 7) .... a teacher. He 8) .... never late for school, and when the children 9) .... he 10) .... very angry. The children 11) .... lessons every day and they always 12) .... homework from their teachers, but sometimes they 13) .... it. When they 14) .... their homework, Maria 15) .... them play with their friends.

1. Present Simple - Present Continuous

4 Now ask and answer questions about the text.

eg. Does Sandra always get up early in the morning? etc.

5 Look at the table, then ask and answer questions as in the example :

	listen to records	read magazines	eat vegetables	watch TV
Sally	✓		✓	✓
Henry & Ann	✓	✓		✓
You				

1. ....*Does*.... Sally listen to records? ...*Yes, she does.*...
2. .... Sally read magazines?
3. .... Sally eat vegetables?
4. .... Sally watch TV?
5. .... Henry & Ann listen to records?
6. .... Henry & Ann read magazines?
7. .... you eat vegetables?
8. .... you watch TV?

6 Now write what Sally and Henry & Ann do and don't do.

Sally ....

Henry & Ann ....

7 Add -ing to the following verbs and put them into the correct column.

run, swim, drive, play, lie, die, read, travel, cycle, put, ride, drink, write, fly, take, cut, sleep

+ ing	ie ➡ y + ing	e ➡ ing	double consonant + ing
playing			

5

1. Present Simple - Present Continuous

8 Choose a verb from the list and complete the text.

read, sleep, eat, sail, cry, drink, run, sing, play, fish, sit

Laura 1) *is sitting* under a sunshade. Two boys 2) .... round a sandcastle while their father 3) .... a newspaper. Tom 4) .... Coke. Two girls 5) .... ice-cream while their mother 6) .... along with the radio. Some boys 7) .... football near a man who 8) .... Jim 9) .... On his right a baby 10) .... Some people 11) .... past the beach.

9 Ask and answer questions about the text above.

eg. Is Laura running? No she isn't. She's sitting under a sunshade. etc

10 Choose a time expression from the list to complete each sentence.

at the moment, tonight, every day, never, always, now

1. She ...*never*... eats meat. She's a vegetarian.
2. Mother is baking a cake ....
3. They are going to a party ....
4. She .... goes to the gym on Saturdays.
5. He drives to work ....
6. She is playing the piano ....

11 Put the verbs in brackets into Present Simple or Present Continuous.

1. She ...*studies*.... (study) every evening.
2. He .... (dance) with Mary now.
3. They .... (get) married next week.
4. She usually .... (take) the bus to school.
5. Her husband never .... (remember) her birthday.
6. We .... (watch) a film on television at the moment.

12 Put the verbs in brackets into Present Simple or Present Continuous.

Chris is asking Kim about her holiday arrangements.

1. Where ...*are*... you ...*going*? ..... (go)
2. How .... you .... there? (get)
3. What time .... the plane .... ? (leave)
4. When .... it .... in Cairo? (arrive)
5. Where .... you .... when you get there? (stay)
6. Why .... you .... to go there? (want)
7. .... you .... a camera with you? (take)

1. Present Simple - Present Continuous

13 Put the verbs in brackets into Present Simple or Present Continuous.

Caller: Good morning, 1) *is* (be) Mr Green there?
Man: No, he 2) .... (not/be) here. He 3) .... (work) at the moment. He usually 4) .... (work) until 4 p.m.
Caller: What about Mrs Green? Where 5) .... (be) she?
Man: She 6) .... (do) the shopping. She always 7) .... (do) the shopping on Thursday afternoons.
Caller: Where 8) .... (be) the children?
Man: They 9) .... (play) football. They always 10) .... (play) football after school.
Caller: How 11) .... (you/know) all this? Who are you?
Man: I 12) .... (be) the burglar!

14 Complete the dialogue using the verbs in brackets in the correct form.

A: Why 1) *don't you finish* (you/not/finish) your homework and come and watch TV?
B: Because I 2) .... (not/understand) it. It is too difficult.
A: Why 3) .... (you/not/ask) your teacher to explain it?
B: Because I 4) .... (not/like) him.
A: And why 5) .... (you/not/like) him?
B: Well, he 6) .... (always/shout) at me.
A: Why 7) .... (he/shout) at you?
B: Well, I 8) .... (not/work) in class and I 9) .... (not/do) my homework.
A: Well, no wonder he 10) .... (shout) at you. Give me your book now. We'll try and do it together.

15 Put the words in brackets in the correct place in the sentences.

1. I (A) *always* keep (B) .... my room tidy. (always)
2. Do you (A) .... go (B) .... on holiday in winter? (sometimes)
3. (A) .... he (B) .... helps with the housework. (never)
4. She (A) .... plays (B) .... cards. (rarely)
5. Does he (A) .... visit (B) .... his friends? (often)
6. They (A) .... don't (B) .... eat sweets. (often)
7. We (A) .... eat (B) .... a lot of vegetables. (usually)
8. You (A) .... must (B) .... tell lies. (never)
9. She (A) .... can (B) .... answer the teacher's questions. (always)

1. Present Simple - Present Continuous

16 Put the verbs in brackets into Present Simple or Present Continuous.

It 1) *is* (be) winter and the snow 2) .... (fall). It usually 3) .... (snow) in January here. Betty and James 4) .... (play) in the garden. They 5) .... (build) a snowman and they 6) .... (throw) snowballs. They 7) .... (like) the snow very much! Their mother and father 8) .... (not/like) it. They always 9) .... (stay) in the house when it is cold. Mother usually 10) .... (watch) TV and Father 11) .... (listen) to the radio or 12) .... (read) a book. At the moment they 13) .... (sit) in the living-room. Mother 14) .... (write) a letter and Father 15) .... (read) a book.

Oral Activity 1

The teacher divides the class into two teams. Then students look at Ex. 16. Team A asks questions while Team B, with books closed, tries to answer them. After five questions change the roles of the teams. Each correct answer gets 1 point. The team with the most points is the winner.

Team A S1 : Is it summer?
Team B S1 : No, it isn't. It's winter.
Team A S2 : Does it snow in July?
Team B S2 : No, it doesn't. It snows in January etc.

Oral Activity 2

The teacher divides the class into two teams and chooses a leader. He / She then gives the leader a piece of paper with a key sentence on it. The leader looks at the key sentence and gives the class some hints about it. The teams ask questions in turn until they find the key sentence. The team that finds it first is the winner.

Key sentences : She is cleaning the floor. / He is reading in the living-room, etc.

(Key sentence : She is cleaning the floor.)
Leader : It's a woman. She is in the kitchen.
Team A S1 : Is she cooking?
Leader : No, she isn't.
Team B S1 : Is she washing the dishes?
Leader : No, she isn't.
Team A S2 : Is she cleaning the floor?
Leader : Yes, she is.

Team A is the winner. The teacher chooses another leader and you can play the game again.

Writing Activity 1

Write 4 things you **usually, often, always** do and another 4 you don't do.

Writing Activity 2

Find a picture from a magazine and write what the people in it are doing at the moment.

2. Past Simple – Present Perfect

Past Simple : verb + ed	Present Perfect : have + past participle
Past Simple is used :	**Present Perfect is used :**
1. for actions which happened at a **stated time** in the past. He **sold** his car two weeks ago. (When? Two weeks ago.)	1. for actions which happened at an **unstated time** in the past. He **has sold** his car. (When? We don't know.)
2. to express a **past state** or **habit**. When she **was** young she **lived** in a small flat.	2. to express actions which have **finished** so **recently** that there's evidence in the present. He **has just painted** the room. (The paint is wet.)
3. for past actions which happened **one after the other**. She **put on** her coat, **took** her bag and **left** the house.	3. for actions which started in the past and **continue up to the present**. She **has lived** in this house for two years. (She still lives in this house.) **BUT :** He **lived** in Australia for one year. (He doesn't live in Australia now.)
4. for a past action whose **time is not mentioned** and which is **not connected with the present**. I **saw** Elvis Presley. (I won't see him again; he's dead. – period of time now finished)	4. for a past action whose **time is not mentioned** but which is **connected with the present**. I'**ve met** Madonna. (I may meet her again; she's still alive. – period of time not finished yet)

2. Past Simple - Present Perfect

Time adverbs and expressions used with Past Simple:	Time adverbs and expressions used with Present Perfect:
yesterday, last week/month/year/ Monday etc, ago, how long ago, just now, then, when, in 1980 etc.	just, ever, never, always, already, yet, for, since, so far, how long, recently, today, this week/month/year, once, several times etc.

17 Add -(e)d to the verbs and put them in the correct column, then read them out.

cry, stay, stop, hate, taste, prefer, fry, dance, like, type, plan, annoy, destroy, pray, phone, beg, try, tip, play, study, travel, enjoy, empty, tidy

-e ➡ +d	double consonant + ed	consonant + y ➡ ied	vowel + y ➡ +ed
hated	stopped	cried	stayed

18 Add -(e)d to the verbs and put them in the correct column, then read them out.

add, wash, rain, need, help, want, count, rob, open, work, marry, close, love, end, invite, laugh, hope, kiss

/ɪd/	/t/	/d/
after /t/,/d/	after /k/,/s/,/tʃ/,/f/,/p/,/ʃ/	after other sounds
added	worked	opened

Special points

- **Since** is used to express a starting point. — I've known Ann **since** October.
- **For** is used to express a period of time. — I've known Ann **for** two months.
- **Yet** is used in questions and negations. — Have you met him **yet**? I haven't met him **yet**.
- **Already** is used in statements and questions. — I've **already** posted the letters.
- **Just** + Present Perfect — I've **just called** the doctor.
- **Just now** + Past Simple — He left **just now**.

19 Fill in: "since", "for", "already", "just" or "yet".

1. John has ...*just*... finished his homework, so his books are still on the table.
2. I haven't seen Sarah .... 1990.
3. Have you .... finished eating? I haven't even started ....
4. We've lived here .... ten years.
5. He's .... come back from jogging and he's a bit tired.

2. Past Simple - Present Perfect

have gone to / have been to / have been in

He's gone to London. (He hasn't come back yet. He is still in London.)
He's been to Paris once. (He's visited Paris. He's back now.) (Present Perfect of the verb "to go")
I've been in Athens for a month. (I am in Athens.) (Present Perfect of the verb "to be")

20 Fill in : has - have been in/to, has - have gone to.

Gina : Hello Paul. Are you enjoying yourself in Rome?
Paul : Oh, yes.
Gina : Which places 1) *have* you *been to* since you arrived?
Paul : Well, I 2) .... Rome for two weeks now so I 3) .... a lot of places, like the Colosseum, some museums and the Vatican.
Gina : Where are your friends today?
Paul : Mark and Jim 4) .... a travel agent's to buy tickets for the plane and they haven't come back yet. Mark says he 5) .... Rome too long. He 6) .... Capri before but Jim and Sean 7) .... (not) any islands, so I think we will go to Sardinia. Sean 8) .... the hotel to sleep.
Gina : Well, I'm leaving now. My parents 9) .... the hospital to see my uncle. He 10) .... hospital for a week. See you later!

21 Fill in the blanks with time adverbs or expressions from the list below:

so far, how long, just, for, since, how long ago, yet, this week, ago, just now, already

1. They got married a month *ago*.
2. He hasn't called us ....
3. I've had this car .... a year.
4. He has .... left.
5. She's typed three letters ....
6. She's .... cooked dinner.
7. .... have you been in Rome?
8. The boss came ....
9. Carol has been to the cinema twice ....
10. .... did he move house?
11. I've studied Maths .... 1991.
12. Peter has been here .... 5 o'clock.

2. Past Simple - Present Perfect

22 Put the verbs in brackets into Present Perfect or Past Simple.

1. A: How long 1) ...*have you had*... (you / have) your car?
   B: I 2) .... (have) it since Christmas. I 3) .... (buy) it from my uncle.
2. A: 4) .... (you /see) that film before?
   B: Yes, I 5) .... (see) it when I 6) .... (be) in London.
3. A: How long 7) .... (you / be) ill?
   B: I 8) .... (be) ill since I 9) .... (eat) that meal.
4. A: When 10) .... (Ann / move) into her new house?
   B: She 11) .... (move) in a month ago. I 12) .... (not / visit) her yet,
   but I 13) ....(arrange) to meet her this week.

23 Put the verbs in brackets into Past Simple.

Many years ago people 1) ..*believed*.. (believe) that some women 2) .... (be) witches. These women 3) .... (not/live) in big cities. They 4) .... (live) in small villages. People 5) .... (think) they 6) .... (behave) strangely because they 7) .... (make) unusual medicines from plants and they 8) .... (not/act) like other people. They 9) .... (say) that they 10) .... (not/walk) but that they 11) .... (fly) on brooms. Do you believe in witches?

24 Ask and answer about Anna and yourself as in the example:

	met a famous person	cooked a foreign meal	had a bad dream	visited a foreign country	been to the theatre
Anna	never	once	several times	recently	many times
You					

1. ...*Has Anna ever met a famous person? No, she has never met a famous person.*........
2. ....
3. ....
4. ....
5. ....
6. Have you ....
7. ....
8. ....
9. ....
10. ....

2. Past Simple - Present Perfect

25) Fill in Present Simple or Present Perfect.

I 1) *have known* (know) Timmy for a long time. We always 2) .... (play) together. Timmy 3) .... (not/can) read or write because he 4) .... (never/be) to school. He 5) .... (have) long brown hair since he was born. He 6) .... (live) in our house for five years. My parents 7) .... (take) care of him while I 8) .... (be) at school. Timmy 9) .... (not/work); actually he 10) .... (never/have) a job. This 11) .... (not/be) strange because Timmy 12) .... (be) my dog.

26) Fill in Past Simple or Present Perfect.

My best friend is called Alison. We 1) *have known* (know) each other since we 2) .... (be) five years old. We 3) .... (always / share) our problems and our troubles, but we 4) .... (also / enjoy) good times together and 5) .... (spend) many hours laughing together. We 6) .... (live) next door to each other before Alison 7) .... (move) to London. I 8) .... (visit) her many times since then. She 9) .... (just / buy) a new house but I 10) .... (not / see) it yet.

27) Use Present S., Present Cont. and Present Perfect to complete the letter.

Dear Sir,

My name 1) *is* (be) Carol Albert and I 2) .... (write) to you about the advertisement in today's newspaper for the secretarial post. I 3) .... (leave) school and at present I 4) .... (study) shorthand and typing at night school. My typing speed 5) .... (be) 60 wpm and my shorthand speed 6) .... (be) 80 wpm. I 7) .... (take) courses in Computer Studies, Accounting and Office Management and I 8) .... (feel) that these courses 9) .... (give) me a lot of experience for the post you 10) .... (advertise). I 11) .... (hope) that you will consider my application. I 12) .... (enclose) a C.V. with my personal details and other information which I 13) .... (think) may interest you. I 14) .... (look) forward to hearing from you very soon.

Yours faithfully,
Carol Albert

2. Past Simple - Present Perfect

28 Put the verbs in brackets into Present Perfect or Past Simple.

Mr Briggs is away on business and he is phoning his wife to see how she is.

Mr Briggs: Hello, darling. How are you? Is everything okay?
Mrs Briggs: I'm fine. I 1) **'ve been** (be) very busy since you 2) .... (leave).
Mr Briggs: What 3) .... (you/do) so far?
Mrs Briggs: I 4) .... (do) the shopping, I 5) .... (wash) and I 6) .... (iron) all the clothes, I 7) .... (clean) the house and I 8) .... (go) to the dentist's. Oh, and yesterday I 9) .... (speak) to a builder about the garage.
Mr Briggs: A builder? The garage? What 10) .... (happen) to the garage?
Mrs Briggs: Well, the garage wall 11) .... (fall down) two days ago.
Mr Briggs: WHAT?????
Mrs Briggs: I.. I 12) .... (not/finish) yet. We, well, I 13) .... (have) a little accident... but I 14) .... (take) the car to the garage to be repaired.
Mr Briggs: Accident? Car? Oh no! You 15) .... (not / crash) my new car into the garage wall?
Mrs Briggs: Er, well, yes! I 16) .... (not / want) to tell you, but that's exactly what 17) .... (happen).

29 Put the verbs in brackets into Past Simple or Present Perfect.

1. A: Last night I .... **saw** .... (see) "The Bodyguard" at the cinema.
   B: Oh, I .... (already / see) it twice.
2. A: Do you know that Mrs Jones .... (work) here for sixteen years?
   B: I thought she .... (start) working here ten years ago.
3. A: .... (you / ever / meet) anyone famous?
   B: Well, I .... (see) Jane Fonda.
   A: Really? I .... (meet) her father, Henry Fonda, once. But he is dead now.
4. A: Yesterday I .... (leave) the house and .... (catch) the train. Then I .... (realise) that my keys .... (be) in the house.
   B: Oh no! That .... (happen) to me before. What .... (you / do)?
   A: I .... (call) the locksmith.
5. A: I .... (already / make) the beds and I .... (just / sweep) the floor, but I .... (not / start) the ironing yet.
   B: Don't worry. I .... (do) it yesterday.
6. A: How long ago .... (you / begin) painting?
   B: Ten years ago. I .... (recently / complete) a painting that the National Gallery .... (ask) me to do a year ago.
7. A: Why are you so happy?
   B: I .... (just / pass) my driving test!
8. A: .... (you / always / have) long hair, Julie?
   B: No, when I was young my hair .... (be) very short.

2. Past Simple - Present Perfect

9. A: On Monday my father .... (give) me £20.
   B: That's wonderful!
   A: No it isn't. I .... (already / spend) it.
10. A: What .... (happen)? Why is the room full of smoke?
    B: I .... (just / cook) your dinner, dear.
    A: Well, I'm not that hungry.

30 Look at the pictures and the list of verbs, then fill in the blanks with Past Simple.

be, begin, become, stop, try, can, crash, fall, see, tell, rescue, take, give, make, arrive, thank

Two men 1) *were* at sea in a small motor boat. It 2) .... to rain and the sea 3) .... very rough. Suddenly the engine 4) .... The men 5) .... but they 6) .... (not) start it again. Then a huge wave 7) .... against the boat and the two men 8) .... into the cold sea. Luckily there 9) .... a big ship nearby and the captain 10) .... the two men. He immediately 11) .... some of his crew to get a lifeboat and save the men. The crew in the lifeboat 12) .... the two men and 13) .... them onto their ship. One of the crew 14) .... the men blankets and 15) .... them hot drinks. When they 16) .... at the harbour the two men 17) .... the captain of the ship and his crew for saving their lives.

Oral Activity 3

The teacher divides the class into two teams and gives them a sentence. The teams in turn ask questions based on the teacher's sentence. Each correct question gets 1 point. The team with the most points is the winner.

Possible sentences : I bought her a present - I went on holiday last summer - The policeman caught the burglar - She moved house, etc.

Teacher :   I went on holiday last summer.   Team B S1 :   Did you enjoy it?
Team A S1 :   Where did you go?   Team A S2 :   Where did you stay? etc.

2. Past Simple - Present Perfect

Oral Activity 4

The teacher divides the class into two teams and starts saying adverbs which take either Past Simple or Present Perfect. The teams in turn make sentences using the adverbs. Each correct sentence gets 1 point. The team with the most points is the winner.

Teacher :	just
Team A S1 :	I've just seen a cat.
Teacher :	never
Team B S1 :	He's never travelled by plane.
Teacher :	last week
Team A S2 :	I went on an excursion last week.
Teacher :	how long ago
Team B S2 :	How long ago have you been in Athens?
Teacher :	No! How long ago did you go to Athens? Team B doesn't get a point.

Oral Activity 5

The teacher divides the class into two teams and writes a list of irregular verbs on the board. The teams in turn make sentences using verbs from the list in Past Simple. Each correct sentence gets 1 point. The team with the most points is the winner.

List: meet, drive, break, go, eat, drink, leave, buy, give, take, write, read, lose, see, come, have, be, find, sing etc.

Team A S1 : I **met** Tom yesterday.
Team B S1 : He **drove** to work yesterday.
Team A S2 : He **broke** an expensive vase last night, etc.

Oral Activity 6

The teacher divides the class into two teams and writes a list of verbs on the board. The teams in turn make up a story using verbs from the list in Past Simple. Each correct sentence gets 1 point. The team with the most points is the winner.

List: get up, eat, have, get dressed, leave, drive, arrive, be closed, not know, get into, turn on, listen, find out, be

Team A S1 : Philip **got up** at 7 o'clock yesterday morning.
Team B S1 : He **ate** his breakfast.
Team A S2 : Then he **had** a shower etc.

Writing Activity 3

Use the verbs from the list in Oral Activity 6 and write a story.

Writing Activity 4

Write 5 sentences saying what you have done or haven't done today.

Writing Activity 5

Write a paragraph about what you did yesterday. (60 - 80 words)

3. Adjectives – Adverbs – Comparisons

Adjectives

Adjectives **describe nouns**; they say "what kind" a noun is. Adjectives have the same form in both singular and plural number and normally come before nouns and after "be".
That car is **fast**. (What kind of car? A fast one.)
She's got three **lovely** cats.

Adverbs

Adverbs **describe verbs**; they explain **how** (adverbs of manner), **where** (adverbs of place), **when** (adverbs of time) or **how often** (adverbs of frequency) something happens.
He drives **carelessly**. (How does he drive? Carelessly.)

We usually form an **adverb** by adding **-ly** to an adjective. eg. slow - slow**ly**. Some adverbs are the same as their adjectives: hard, fast, early, daily, late, monthly. eg. He runs **fast**. He is a **fast** runner. Some adverbs are irregular. eg. good - well

31 Write the correct adverbs.

➡ ly	✗ ➡ ly	consonant + ✗ ➡ ily
wide .... *widely*	possible	busy ....
dangerous	simple	heavy ....
sad	terrible	happy ....

32 Put the words from the list below into the correct column.

bad, well, early, angrily, easily, noisy, quick, quietly, daily, tidy, carelessly, slowly, hard, late, large, monthly, careful, happily

Adjectives	Adverbs	Adjectives & Adverbs
bad	*angrily*	*well*

3. Adjectives - Adverbs - Comparisons

33 Put the adverbs from the list below into the correct column.

always, yesterday, on Sunday, here, last year, easily, now, usually, often, there, away, everywhere, happily, carefully, seldom, badly

How	Where	When	How often
adverbs of manner	adverbs of place	adverbs of time	adverbs of frequency
easily,			

Order of Adjectives

1. "Opinion" adjectives (bad, good etc) go before "fact" adjectives (old, red etc).
   She bought a **beautiful red** dress.

2. When there are two or more "fact" adjectives, they go in the following order:

	size	age	shape	colour	origin	material	noun
This is a	large	old	rectangular	brown	French	wooden	bed.

34 Put the adjectives in the right order.

1. a new/woollen/red/smart/hat ... *a smart new red woollen hat*
2. a(n) modern/luxurious/Italian car
3. two silk/long/blue/beautiful dresses
4. a pair of leather/old/brown shoes
5. a(n) stone/English/small/church
6. a green/fantastic/Japanese/large motorbike
7. a(n) old/English/heavy dictionary
8. a plastic/blue/little spoon
9. a new/wooden/black/huge/ armchair
10. a gold/tiny/round/Russian/coin

Order of Adverbs

1. **Adverbs of frequency** (often, usually etc) go after auxiliary verbs but before main **verbs.** eg. She **is never** late. He **never comes** late.

2. When there are more than two adverbs, they go in the following order:

	manner	place	time
She sat	lazily	by the pool	all day.

3. When there is a verb of movement, then the order is:

	place	manner	time
He walks	home	quickly	every afternoon.

3. Adjectives - Adverbs - Comparisons

35 Underline the correct word, adjective or adverb.

1. The children played quiet / <u>quietly</u>.
2. It was raining heavy / heavily yesterday.
3. She gave it a careful / carefully look.
4. She speaks perfect / perfectly German.
5. Have you seen Rebecca recent / recently?
6. He's a slow / slowly runner.
7. She sings good / well.
8. She bought a nice / nicely dress.

36 Rewrite the sentences in the correct order.

1. he went/in the morning/to school/by bicycle ... *He went to school by bicycle in the morning.*
2. at breakfast/I/drink coffee/always
3. goes to work/by bus/never/Sam
4. at school/yesterday/hard/I worked
5. his books/often/forgets/Tom
6. quietly/someone knocked/at midnight/at the door
7. for an hour/in the queue/patiently/he waited
8. he goes/often/abroad/on business
9. rarely/see foxes/you/in these woods

Comparisons

Did you catch any **big** fish today?

Yes, they are **bigger than** the ones I caught yesterday. They are **as big as** baby elephants.

Fishing is not allowed here and I'm the warden, you know.

And I am **the biggest** liar **in** the world.

Adjectives of:	Positive	Comparative	Superlative
one syllable	tall	tall**er** (than)	the tall**est** (of/in)
two syllables **ending in -er, -ly, -y, -w**	happy friendly	happ**ier** (than) friendl**ier** (than)	the happ**iest** (of/in) the friendl**iest** (of/in)
two or more syllables	modern beautiful	**more** modern (than) **more** beautiful (than)	the **most** modern (of/in) the **most** beautiful (of/in)

3. Adjectives - Adverbs - Comparisons

Spelling

Adjectives ending in:		
e + r / st	x ➡ ier / iest	one stressed vowel between two consonants - double the consonant
large-larger-largest	heavy-heavier-heaviest	big-bigger-biggest

37 Fill in the blanks with the correct comparative and superlative forms.

1. thin — thinner — thinnest
2. long
3. wet
4. dangerous
5. difficult
6. easy
7. exciting
8. hot

Comparison of Adverbs

	Positive	Comparative	Superlative
adverbs with the same form as adjectives	fast	faster	the fastest
two-syllable adverbs ending in -ly	early	earlier	the earliest
two-syllable or compound adverbs (adjective + -ly) (clear - clearly)	often clearly	more often more clearly	the most often the most clearly

38 Fill in the blanks with the correct comparative and superlative forms.

1. late — later — latest
2. loudly
3. often
4. politely
5. hard
6. carefully
7. clearly
8. fast
9. fluently
10. noisily

Irregular Forms

Positive	Comparative	Superlative
good/well	better	best
bad/badly	worse	worst
much	more	most
many/a lot of	more	most
little	less	least
far	further/farther	furthest/farthest

a) **further / farther** (adv) = longer (in distance)
I have to walk **further / farther** than him.
further (adj) = more
For **further** information, see the secretary.

b) **very** + positive degree
   much + comparative degree
   It's **very** cold today.
   It's **much** colder here than in Athens.

3. Adjectives - Adverbs - Comparisons

39 Fill in the blanks with the correct comparative and superlative forms.

1. bad — *worse* — *worst*
2. gently
3. many
4. little
5. clever
6. good
7. funny
8. useful
9. sad
10. far

40 Fill in the blanks as in the example:

I went on holiday last year but it was a disaster! My hotel room was 1) *smaller than* (small) the one in the photograph in the brochure. I think it was 2) .... (small) room .... the hotel. The weather was terrible too. It was 3) .... (cold) in England. The beach near the hotel was very dirty – it was 4) .... (dirty) all the beaches on the island. The food was 5) .... (expensive) .... I expected and I didn't have enough money. One day I went shopping in a big department store and I broke a vase. It was 6) .... (expensive) vase .... the whole shop. But 7) .... (bad) thing .... all was that I lost my passport and I couldn't go back home. It was 8) .... (horrible) holiday .... my life.

41 Fill in the blanks as in the example:

M: I'm happy I'm not a woman!
W: Why?
M: Men are 1) *better than* (good) women.
W: But you are 2) .... (stupid) person I know!
M: Don't be horrible. Men are 3) .... (intelligent) .... women. They are 4) .... (logical) and 5) .... (good) cooks .... women are!
W: Your ideas are 6) .... (old-fashioned) .... mine. I think women are 7) .... (clever).

They are 8) .... (sensible) and 9) .... (practical) .... men are – and men are 10) .... (bad) drivers than women because women are 11) .... (patient).
M: But men are 12) .... (athletic).
W: Oh, please. Let's talk about something else. This is 13) .... (ridiculous) conversation I have ever had!

3. Adjectives - Adverbs - Comparisons

42 Fill in: very or much.

London is becoming a 1) ...... *very* ... popular place for American tourists. All the big attractions are now 2) .... busy in the summer months. The crowds of tourists around places like Buckingham Palace are 3) .... bigger than they were a few years ago. Sales of postcards and other souvenirs are 4) .... higher now than in past years. This is 5) .... good news for the British tourist industry.

43 Write sentences as in the example comparing the six cars.

| fast | cheap | dangerous | big | expensive |
| safe | small | attractive | slow | comfortable |

1. B.M.W. : *I think a B.M.W. is more comfortable than a Volkswagen. I don't think it's the most attractive of all though.*
2. Mercedes : ....
3. Rolls Royce : ....
4. Fiat : ....
5. Jaguar : ....
6. Volkswagen : ....

Types of Comparisons

The red book is **as old as** the blue book but it **isn't as thick as** the blue one.

The ring is **less expensive than** the necklace. The earrings are **the least expensive of** all.

The more he eats, **the fatter** he gets.

1. **as** ...(positive)... **as** **not so / as** ... (positive)... **as**	Paul is **as heavy as** Tom. Jane is **not as / so tall as** Mary.
2. **less** ...(positive)... **than** **the least** ...(positive)... **of/in**	Betty is **less hard-working than** Kate but Jean is **the least hard-working of** all.
3. **the + comparative...**, **the + comparative**	**The harder** you work, **the more** money you earn.

3. Adjectives - Adverbs - Comparisons

44 Fill in the blanks as in the example:

1. (fast / slow) Peter is a *faster* swimmer *than* Paul. Mary isn't *as fast as* Paul. She is *the slowest* swimmer *of* all.

2. (long) The dog has got .... ears .... the cat. The cat's ears aren't .... the dog's. The rabbit has got .... ears .... all.

3. (cheap / expensive) The green hat is .... the red hat. The yellow hat is .... the green hat but the red hat is .... all.

4. (big / small) A bird is .... a butterfly but .... a goat. A butterfly isn't .... a bird. A butterfly is .... all.

45 Use the adjectives and write comparisons as in the example:

1. **heavy, dangerous, fierce, fast**

An elephant *is heavier than a tiger*.
An elephant *is less dangerous than a tiger*.
A tiger is *fiercer than an elephant*.
An elephant isn't *as fast as a tiger*.

2. **expensive, cheap, slow, comfortable**

A car is ....
A bicycle is ....
A car isn't ....
A bicycle is ....

3. **dirty, friendly, intelligent, noisy**

A rat is ....
A rat is ....
A dog is ....
A rat isn't ....

3. Adjectives - Adverbs - Comparisons

46 Write comparisons for the following as in the example :

1. Snakes are dangerous. *Yes, but tigers are more dangerous.*
2. Spain is a hot country.
3. Pearls are expensive.
4. Dogs are intelligent.
5. Greek is a difficult language.
6. Travelling by bus is safe.

Oral Activity 7

The teacher divides the class into two teams and writes a list of adjectives on the board. Then he / she asks the students to look at the pictures and compare items from A with items from B using the adjectives on the board. Each correct sentence gets 1 point. The team with the most points is the winner.

List : expensive, intelligent, interesting, tasty, big, exciting, fierce, dangerous, beautiful, short, comfortable, healthy, etc.

Team A S1 : A chair is less comfortable than an armchair.
Team B S1 : Tigers are more dangerous than snakes.
Team A S2 : Jane has got shorter hair than Jill, etc.

Writing Activity 6

Use the adjectives **hard-working**, **funny**, **tall**, **polite**, **friendly**, **young**, **athletic** and **helpful** and compare yourself to your friend.
eg. I'm more **athletic** than my friend, etc.

4. Will – Be Going To

There's **going to be** a terrible snowstorm. You**'ll have** to stay the night with us.

In that case I**'ll phone** my husband.

Good idea. He **will probably be** worried if you don't phone him.

Oh no! It's not that! I**'m going to ask** him to bring my nightclothes here for me.

We use **will** and **be going to** to talk about the future.

Will is used :

1. **to talk about things we are not sure about or we haven't decided yet.**
   I**'ll** probably **buy** a new car. (I'm not sure yet.)

2. **to express hopes, fears, threats, on-the-spot decisions, offers, promises, warnings, predictions, comments** etc. especially with: expect, hope, believe, I'm afraid, I'm sure, I know, I think, probably etc.
   I think it **will be** sunny tomorrow. (prediction)

3. **to express a prediction or a future action or event which may or may not happen.**
   I think you **will pass** the test. (prediction)
   He **will be** twenty next year. (future event)
   She **will** probably **phone** later. (prediction)

Be Going To is used :

1. **to talk about things we are sure about or we have already decided to do in the near future.**
   I**'m going to buy** a new car. (I've decided it.)

2. **to express intention and plans.**
   Now that I've got the money, I**'m going to buy** a new dress. (intention)
   I**'m going to get** some more training so I can get a better job. (plan)

3. **when we can see (evidence) that something is going to happen.**
   Watch out! We**'re going to have** an accident. (We can see a car coming.)
   It**'s going to rain**. (We can see dark clouds in the sky.)

Time expressions used with will and be going to :

tomorrow, tonight, next week/month/year, in two days, the day after tomorrow, soon, in a week/month etc.

4. Will - Be Going To

47 Fill in: will or be going to, then identify the speech situations (sure, not yet sure).

1. ... *not yet sure* ...

I ... *will move* ... (move) into a better house if I get a job.

2. ....

He .... (play) tennis.

3. ....

They .... (probably/buy) a new car.

4. ....

I think he .... (be) angry when he sees the cat.

5. ....

They .... (fight).

6. ....

He .... (take) a picture.

Will	Shall
is used to express predictions, warnings, offers, promises, threats, requests, suggestions, on-the-spot decisions, opinions, hopes and fears (especially with words such as: think, expect, suppose, hope, believe, know and probably). I expect she **will** come early. (prediction)	**is used with I or We in questions, suggestions and offers.** **Shall we** go by train? (suggestion) **Shall I** help you with your bags? (offer)

48 Fill in: will, won't or shall.

Larry: 1) .. *Shall* .. we go for a picnic tomorrow?
Sue: Yes. That's a good idea. I 2) .... make some sandwiches.
Larry: OK. And I 3) .... bring some lemonade.
Sue: 4) .... I buy some cheese?
Larry: I don't really like cheese.
Sue: I 5) .... buy any cheese then. I 6) .... bring some fruit instead.
Larry: I think it 7) .... be sunny tomorrow so I 8) .... probably wear my shorts. I 9) .... take a pullover.
Sue: Well, I think I 10) .... take mine. It is still cold in the mornings.
Larry: 11) .... I invite Bob and Linda?
Sue: That's a good idea. It 12) .... be nice if they come.

4. Will - Be Going To

Study these points:

1. We use **Present Continuous** rather than "be going to" for things which are **definitely arranged** to happen in the future.
   They**'re having** a party next week. (It's all arranged. Invitations have already been sent.)
   They**'re going to have** a party in two weeks. (They've decided it but it hasn't been arranged yet.)

2. We use **Present Simple** for **timetables**, **programmes** etc.   Our plane **leaves** at 10.30 a.m.

3. We do not use the Future tense after the words **while**, **before**, **until**, **as soon as**, **if** (conditional) and **when** (time conjunction). However, we can use **when + will**, if **when** is a question word.
   Call me **when** you arrive.   BUT   When will you be ready?

4. With the verbs **go** and **come** we often use Present Continuous rather than "be going to".
   I**'m going** out tonight.   RATHER THAN   I**'m going to go** out tonight.

49 Fill in Present Cont. or be going to, then identify the speech situations.

fixed arrangement - something already decided

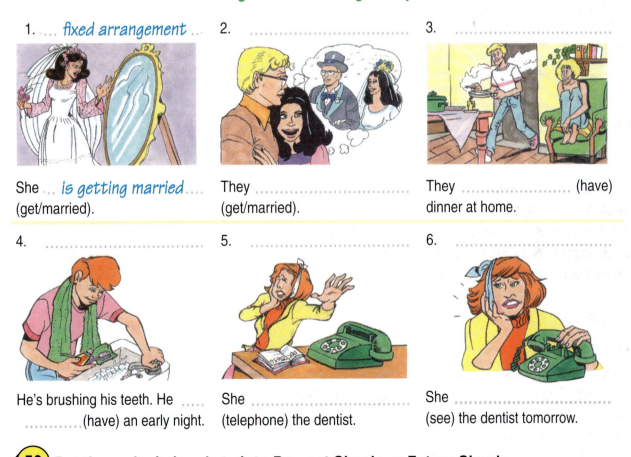

1. ..*fixed arrangement*..
She ..*is getting married*.. (get/married).

2. ....
They .... (get/married).

3. ....
They .... (have) dinner at home.

4. ....
He's brushing his teeth. He .... (have) an early night.

5. ....
She .... (telephone) the dentist.

6. ....
She .... (see) the dentist tomorrow.

50 Put the verbs in brackets into Present Simple or Future Simple.

1. We ....*will leave*........ (leave) as soon as he ....*arrives*........ (arrive).
2. He says he .... (telephone) us before he .... (leave) the airport.
3. She .... (stay) at home until she .... (feel) better.
4. "When .... (you/visit) them?" "Probably next week."

4. Will - Be Going To

5. When he .... (finish) school he .... (go) to university.
6. I .... (send) you a postcard as soon as I .... (get) there.
7. When .... (she/be) back? | 8. The plane .... (leave) at 7.00.

51 Match the sentences with the pictures, then identify the speech situations.

1. I'll write to you every day!
2. Look at that tree! It's going to fall down.
3. I love cooking. I'm going to be a chef.
4. He's going to paint his house.
5. I'll have two cheeseburgers for lunch.
6. Shall I do the washing-up?
7. Put on your coat or you'll catch cold!
8. Finish your homework or I won't take you to the zoo.
9. Robots will do the housework in the future.

intention, promise, evidence, prediction, offer, threat, warning, on-the-spot decision

1. ....*intention*....

....*He's going to paint his house.*....

2. ....

....

3. ....

....

4. ....

....

5. ....

....

6. ....

....

7. ....

....

8. ....

....

9. ....

....

4. Will - Be Going To

52 Write sentences using be going to, Present Continuous or Present Perfect.

(he / make speech)

1. *He's going to make a speech.*
2. *He's making a speech.*
3. *He has made a speech.*

(he / clean car)

4. ....
5. ....
6. ....

(she / wash the dog)

7. ....
8. ....
9. ....

(she / buy some flowers)

10. ....
11. ....
12. ....

4. Will - Be Going To

53) Fill in: will or be going to.

Julie is planning her summer holiday.

I 1) **'m going to** spend my holiday in Crete because there is a lot to see. I 2) .... travel there by ferry because I enjoy boat trips. I'm not going on my own; my best friend 3) .... come with me and I think my cousin 4) .... come too if I ask her. We 5) .... stay in Hania for two weeks, then we 6) .... go somewhere else. I hope we 7) .... find a hotel easily but if there's any problem, we 8) .... stay at a campsite. We 9) .... swim every day so I 10) .... take a lot of suntan oil with me – I think we 11) .... need it. I am looking forward to this holiday. I'm sure it 12) .... be the best holiday ever.

54) Fill in: be going to or will.

I heard on TV last night that Portsmouth Council 1) **is going to** build a new swimming pool in the centre of town. They 2) .... start work in July and the pool 3) .... probably be finished by September. The Mayor said, "I'm sure the people of Portsmouth 4) .... welcome the new pool. I hope they 5) .... understand the temporary problems which 6) .... be caused in the centre of town." The opposition leader does not seem to like the idea. He 7) .... organise a protest to stop the council wasting public money, and he believes that the majority of the people living in Portsmouth 8) .... support him.

55) Put the verbs in brackets into Present S., Present Cont. or be going to.

1. John is a student. He usually **studies** (study) very hard. He .... (study) Ancient History now. He .... (study) Modern History next year.
2. Julie and Ted often .... (climb) mountains. They .... (climb) Snowdon at the moment. They .... (climb) the Eiger next summer.
3. Mother .... (bake) a cake now. She .... (bake) cakes every Saturday. Next Saturday she .... (bake) a beautiful one for my birthday party.

56) Fill in: shall, will or be going to.

1. A: What do you want for lunch?
   B: I think I 1) **will** have chicken and some salad.
2. A: John has come back from England.
   B: I know. I 2) .... see him tonight.
3. A: I haven't got any money.
   B: I 3) .... lend you some if you want me to.

4. Will - Be Going To

4. A: Ben and I 4) .... get married in April.
   B: Really? Congratulations!
5. A: 5) .... we meet on Sunday?
   B: Sorry, but I 6) .... visit my aunt. She is expecting me.
6. A: Is Dave coming to the party?
   B: Yes, but he 7) .... probably be late.
7. A: Laura is in hospital.
   B: Really? I 8) .... send her some flowers.
8. A: Have you decided where to go on holiday?
   B: Yes, I 9) .... travel round Europe.
9. A: The plants need watering.
   B: I know. I 10) .... water them later.

57 Write what David's plans are for next week. Then write about your plans.

David

Monday:	do his shopping
Tuesday:	correct tests
Wednesday:	buy a new shirt
Thursday:	go to the gym
Friday:	visit Helen
Saturday:	have a party
Sunday:	watch TV

1. *David is going to do his shopping on Monday.*
2. ....
3. ....
4. ....
5. ....
6. ....
7. ....

You

Monday:	*tidy my room*
Tuesday:	....
Wednesday:	....
Thursday:	....
Friday:	....
Saturday:	....
Sunday:	....

1. *I'm going to tidy my room on Monday.*
2. ....
3. ....
4. ....
5. ....
6. ....
7. ....

58 Put the verbs in brackets into Present Cont., Present S., be going to or will.

Sam: 1) ...... *Shall we go* ...... (we/go) to the cinema?
Claire: Sorry, I can't. I 2) .... (go) out with Peter tonight. He 3) .... (pick) me up at 8 o'clock.
Sam: I 4) .... (go) on my own then, or maybe I 5) .... (ring) Sue to see if she 6) .... (want) to come.
Claire: That's a good idea. 7) .... (you/go) to the cinema in Green Street?
   I 8) .... (think) "Batman" is on there.

31

4. Will - Be Going To

Sam: Yes, I 9) .... (probably/go) there. I 10) .... (phone) and see what time the film 11) .... (start).

59 Put the verbs in brackets into Present S., Present Cont. or Future tense.

Gary: What 1) ... *are you planning* ... (you/plan) to do after the exams? 2) .... (you/stay) in London?
Angela: No, I 3) .... (leave) on Saturday. I've bought my ticket already. I 4) .... (visit) my brother in Wales. What 5) .... (you/do)?
Gary: I think I 6) .... (start) looking for a job. I 7) .... (need) some extra money because my mum 8) .... (come) here in August. She 9) .... (stay) with me for a month. I 10) .... (plan) to show her London.
Angela: When exactly 11) .... (she/arrive)?
Gary: Her flight 12) .... (arrive) at Heathrow airport at 4:30 p.m. on August 3rd. I 13) .... (meet) her there.
Angela: You've missed her a lot, haven't you?
Gary: Yes. I 14) .... (look forward) to seeing her.

Oral Activity 8

Look at the following grid:

	Where	When	How	What you/they are going to do/see.
You				
Your friend				

Using Ex. 53 as a model, students work in pairs and plan their holiday including where, when, how they are going and what they are going to do/see.
The teacher moves round the class and helps students plan their trips. After 4-5 minutes some students tell the class about their plans and their partner's plans.

Writing Activity 7

Write a letter to your uncle about a trip you are planning to take. (40 - 60 words)

Revision Exercises I

60 Choose the correct item.

1. What are you cooking? It ...B... very nice!
   A) is smelling   B) smells   C) smelt

2. John .... very hard at the moment.
   A) worked   B) has worked   C) is working

3. .... I help you carry those bags?" "Yes, please."
   A) Shall   B) Will   C) Do

4. I .... a new bike last week.
   A) bought   B) have bought   C) will buy

5. They .... in England for twenty years.
   A) are living   B) live   C) have lived

6. I .... Elvis Presley in 1965.
   A) have seen   B) saw   C) am seeing

7. We always .... fish on Fridays.
   A) are going to eat   B) eat   C) eats

8. "Why have you got those flowers?" "Because I .... my aunt in hospital."
   A) will visit   B) am going to visit   C) visit

9. The children played .... in the garden.
   A) happy   B) happier   C) happily

10. The bigger the car, the .... it is.
    A) fast   B) fastest   C) faster

61 Find the mistake and correct it.

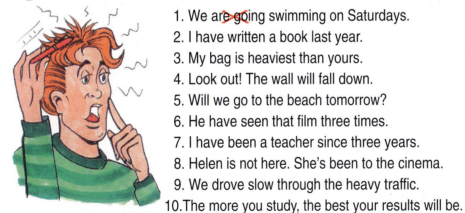

1. We are going swimming on Saturdays.   ..go..
2. I have written a book last year.
3. My bag is heaviest than yours.
4. Look out! The wall will fall down.
5. Will we go to the beach tomorrow?
6. He have seen that film three times.
7. I have been a teacher since three years.
8. Helen is not here. She's been to the cinema.
9. We drove slow through the heavy traffic.
10. The more you study, the best your results will be.

62 Fill in: very or much.

It is (1) ..very.. interesting to go on safari in Africa where it's 2) .... hotter than in other countries. There's also a 3) .... greater variety of animals to see. Lions are 4) .... large animals but elephants are 5) .... bigger. Elephants don't often run 6) .... fast but they're 7) .... stronger than lions. Giraffes are 8) .... taller than lions or elephants and they can run 9) .... fast too. It's 10) .... better to see animals in the jungle than in the zoo!

Revision Exercises I

63 Put the adjectives in brackets into the correct form.

Tom's car
price: £15,000
speed: 110 mph
size: medium
petrol consumption: average
made in 1990

John's car
price: £7,000
speed: 90 mph
size: small
petrol consumption: low
made in 1987

Carol's car
price: £19,000
speed: 130 mph
size: large
petrol consumption: high
made in 1992

Tom's car is 1) ...*more expensive than*... John's (expensive) but Carol's car is 2) .... all (expensive). Tom's car isn't 3) .... Carol's car (big). Carol's car is 4) .... all (big). Carol's car is 5) .... all (modern). John's car is 6) .... all (old). Tom's car is 7) .... Carol's (economical) but John's is 8) .... all (economical). John's car isn't 9) .... Tom's (fast). It is 10) .... Tom's (slow). Carol's car is 11) .... all (fast) but it is 12) .... all (economical).

64 Put the verbs in brackets into Past Simple or Present Perfect.

1. A: How long 1) ..*have you lived*.... (you / live) in America?
   B: I 2) .... (come) here in 1990.
2. A: I 3) .... (just/finish) my composition.
   B: Really? I 4) .... (write) mine yesterday evening.
3. A: I 5) .... (not/see) you for years! When 6) .... (you/leave) school?
   B: Last year. I 7) .... (start) university last September.

65 Fill in: shall, will or be going to.

Alan is going to New York on business tomorrow.

Alan: My plane leaves at 2 o'clock and I haven't got anything ready yet. What 1) *am I going to* do? I 2) .... never be ready on time.
Helen: Well, I 3) .... take the children to school in 5 minutes. Then I 4) .... come back and help you. 5) .... I pack your clothes?
Alan: Okay, thanks. I 6) .... get washed and shaved.
Helen: 7) .... you .... drive into town this morning?
Alan: Yes, I 8) .... collect my ticket in about an hour.
Helen: 8) .... you get me some flour? I 10) .... bake a cake this afternoon.

Revision Exercises I

66 Fill in: has/have been in/to, has/have gone to.

1. A: 1) ...*Have you ever been to*...... France?
   B: No, I haven't, but I'd like to go.
2. A: Do you know where Mum is?
   B: I think she 2) .... the post office to get some stamps.
3. A: Sorry we're late. We 3) .... London for the day.
   B: And you got stuck in a traffic jam, didn't you?
4. A: I'm afraid Sue and Pam can't come with us. They 4) .... visit their grandmother.
   B: She 5) .... hospital for a long time, hasn't she?

67 Complete the text using since or for.

Maria has lived in England 1) *since*.. 1988. She has been married to James 2) .... four years. She has known him 3) .... 1987 when they met in Paris. They have lived in central London 4) .... two years. They have lived at their present address 5) .... last summer. Maria has worked for the French Embassy 6) .... nine months. James and his family have run a small hotel in the heart of London 7) .... many years. James has been the manager 8) .... Christmas, when his father retired. Maria and James have saved a lot of money 9) .... last year, so they are planning to go on a trip to France.

68 Put the verbs in brackets into Present S., Present Cont. or the Future tense.

John: Hello, Gary. Where 1) *are you going* (you/go)?
Gary: To the sports centre. I've got a football training session. Our team 2) .... (go) to France next week. We 3) .... (leave) on Wednesday.
John: Oh, that 4) .... (be) great! How 5) .... (you/get) there?
Gary: We 6) .... (travel) on the ferry. It 7) .... (leave) at 5 o'clock in the morning.
John: How long 8) .... (you/stay) in France?
Gary: About a week. We 9) .... (play) four matches. The first one 10) .... (start) at 3 o'clock on Wednesday afternoon, and the last one 11) .... (finish) at 5 o'clock on the following Tuesday.
John: Do you think you 12) .... (win)?
Gary: Yes, but I have to go now. The coach 13) .... (shout) at me if I'm late for training. I 14) .... (tell) you all about it when I 15) .... (get) back.

69 Fill in: yet, already, just, ago, since, for or how long.

1. Is it really a year ....*since*.. we last had a holiday?
2. I'm afraid I haven't finished my work ....
3. Shakespeare was born over four hundred years ....
4. Paul has .... bought one car, but he's going to buy another one next week.

Revision Exercises I

5. Don't eat that cake! I've .... made it and it's still hot.
6. My sister has been at university .... six months.
7. .... have you known John and Susan?
8. Haven't you typed those letters .... ? I need them now.
9. She's .... cleaned the house and it's only 9 o'clock in the morning.
10. I haven't watched T.V. .... my set broke down.

70 Fill in Present S., Present Cont., Past S., Present Perfect or will.

Peter 1) ...is...... (be) one of my best friends. At the moment he 2) .... (stay) with my family in London. I 3) .... (know) him since I 4) .... (be) a little girl when we 5) .... (play) together after school. Now Peter 6) .... (look) for a job in London. He 7) .... (just/pass) his exams and 8) .... (want) to be a journalist. Tomorrow he 9) .... (have) an interview. I hope he 10) .... (get) the job!

71 Put the words in the correct order to make sentences.

1. never / he / his wife's birthday / forgets .....*He never forgets his wife's birthday.*.....
2. usually / she / wake up / early / doesn't
3. always/ he / has / to travel abroad / wanted
4. rarely / he / at night / goes out
5. they / always / do / can / anything / they want

72 Fill in Present S., Present Cont., Past S., Present Perfect, will or be going to.

My cousin's name 1) ...is...... (be) Sylvie Dupont. She 2) .... (live) in Paris and 3) .... (work) in a café in the centre of the city. She (4) .... (work) there for three years. At the moment her best friend from England 5) .... (stay) with her. She 6) .... (enjoy) her holiday very much. They 7) .... (already/visit) many museums together and they 8) .... (be) to the theatre three times. Next week they 9) .... (see) a film and then they 10) .... (have) dinner at an expensive restaurant. Last Tuesday they 11) .... (go) to a disco with some friends of theirs. They 12) .... (not/come) home until very late. Sylvie 13) .... (be) so tired at work the following day that she 14) .... (spill) coffee all over a customer. She doesn't think she 15) .... (see) him at the café again! In future she 16) .... (not/stay) out so late and she 17) .... (be) more careful while she is serving customers.

5. Present Perfect Continuous

Have you been fighting again? You've lost your front teeth.

No, I haven't lost them, Mum. They are in my pocket!

Form: have / has been + verb -ing

Affirmative	Interrogative	Negative
I have been working	Have I been working?	I have not been working
You have been working	Have you been working?	You have not been working
He has been working	Has he been working?	He has not been working
She has been working	Has she been working?	She has not been working
It has been working	Has it been working?	It has not been working
We have been working	Have we been working?	We have not been working
You have been working	Have you been working?	You have not been working
They have been working	Have they been working?	They have not been working
Short form	**Negative-Interrogative**	**Short form**
I've been working ...	Haven't you been working? ...	I haven't been working ...

73 Put the verbs in brackets into Present Perfect Continuous.

Tim: Hello Joe. What 1) ...*have you been doing*... (you/do)?
Joe: I 2) .... (play) tennis with Helen.
Tim: Who is Helen?
Joe: She's my new girlfriend. I 3) .... (go) out with her for two weeks.
Tim: Does she live here?
Joe: Yes, she 4) .... (live) here for two months.
Tim: Why haven't I met her?
Joe: Because she 5) .... (leave) home early and she 6) .... (come) back late every day for the last six weeks.
Tim: Why 7) .... (she/do) that?
Joe: Because she 8) .... (look for) a job.
Tim: I must meet her some time.
Joe: Well, let's all go out together tomorrow then.

5. Present Perfect Continuous

Present Perfect Continuous is used:	**Present Perfect is used:**
1. for actions which started in the past and continue **up to the present**.  **I've been packing** my case all morning. (I'm still packing.)	1. for actions **recently** completed.  **I've packed** my case. (I've just finished.)
2. for continuous past actions which have **visible results** or effect in the **present**.  They **have been walking** in the rain. (They are wet.)	2. for actions which happened at an **unstated time**.  She **has done** a lot of shopping.
3. to express **irritation, anger, annoyance, explanation** or **criticism**.  **Has** the dog **been chewing on** my slippers? (showing anger)	3. to express personal **experiences** or **changes** which have happened.  **I've put on** a lot of weight.
4. to put **emphasis on duration**, usually with **for, since** or **how long**. I've been typing letters **since** 9 o'clock.	4. to put **emphasis on number**. I've only **typed three** letters since 9 o'clock.
NOTE With the verbs **live, feel** and **work** we can use either Present Perfect or Present Perf. Cont. with no difference in meaning. **I've been living** in London for a year. or **I've lived** in London for a year.	Non-continuous verbs are not used in Present Perfect Cont. (**know, believe, see, like, love, taste, understand, want** etc.) **I've known** her since 1985. (NOT: ~~I've been knowing her since 1985.~~)

5. Present Perfect Continuous

Time adverbs used with Present Perfect Continuous :	Time adverbs and expressions used with Present Perfect :
for, since, how long	just, ever, never, always, already, yet, for, since, so far, how long, recently, today, this week/month/year, once, etc.

74 Identify the speech situations, then complete the sentences.

recently completed action, emphasis on number, unstated time, anger or annoyance, emphasis on duration, personal experience, visible results

1. ...visible results...
I ...have been painting... (paint) my room.

2. ....
They .... (just/got married).

3. ....
She .... (iron) all day.

4. ....
.... (you/cook) again?

5. ....
She .... (have) a haircut.

6. ....
He .... (be) to Africa.

7. ....
They .... (buy) a pet dog.

8. ....
He .... (write) three letters.

9. ....
She .... (write) letters all morning.

5. Present Perfect Continuous

75 Put the verbs in brackets into Present Perfect or Present Perfect Continuous.

1. A: I'm very tired.
   B: That's because you 1) ...*have been working*... (work) too hard.
   A: I know. But at least I 2) .... (finish) my composition.
2. A: You look hot. What 3) .... (you/do)?
   B: I 4) .... (play) tennis with Sarah.
   A: Oh yes. I 5) .... (see) her play before. She's good, isn't she?
   B: Yes, she is. She 6) .... (beat) me five times since the start of the summer.

76 Put the verbs in brackets into Present Perfect or Present Perfect Continuous.

Pam: What are you doing, Ben?
Ben: I 1) ......*'ve been looking through*...... (look through) my old toy box all morning. It brings back lots of memories. Look, I 2) .... (find) my old train set!
Pam: You 3) .... (play) with those trains for over an hour. I 4) .... (watch) you.
Ben: They're great! I 5) .... (not/have) so much fun for years. Look at this one!
Pam: Yes, Ben – it's a very nice train. But 6) .... (you/see) what time it is?
Ben: No... Why?
Pam: It's 10.30. Your boss 7) .... (just/phone) from the office.
Ben: Why?
Pam: He 8) .... (wait) for you all morning. You have an important meeting.
Ben: Oh no! I thought it was Sunday!

77 Fill in the blanks with *for* or *since*.

Tom and Mary have been building a house 1) ...*for*... two years. They have been dreaming of finishing it 2) .... last summer but they have been having problems 3) .... a few months because of the weather. In fact, it has been raining and snowing 4) .... October so they haven't been able to put the roof on yet. This weekend they are trying to put in the windows. They have only been working 5) .... 8 o'clock but they feel like they've been doing it 6) .... hours because it is very difficult. They have been saving up 7) .... a long time but they haven't been able to hire any workmen yet. Tom has been looking for an evening job 8) .... a week and Mary has been working overtime 9) .... Christmas, so they will have enough money soon. They haven't been going out 10) .... they started saving – but when the house is finished they are going to have a big party to celebrate.

5. Present Perfect Continuous

Oral Activity 9

The teacher divides the class into two teams. Students look at the picture and the teacher introduces Mr May.(**Mr May is a strange old man. He doesn't like changes. He has been doing the same things for years.**) Then, looking at the list of verbs and using the picture as a stimulus, students, in turn, suggest what Mr May has been doing. The team which cannot give a sentence or makes a mistake doesn't get a point. The team with the most points is the winner.

List of verbs : read, wear, collect, drink, play, live, etc.

The teacher gives an example and students start the game.
- Teacher : He has been collecting butterflies for ten years.
- Team A S1: He has been reading the same newspaper for thirty years.
- Team B S1: He has been living in the same house for fifty years. etc.

Oral Activity 10

Students compare both pictures, then comment on the first one. eg. Tom didn't have a beard three months ago. Jane was fat. etc. Then students look at the second picture and say what has happened since then. eg. Tom has grown a beard. Jane has lost weight etc.

Writing Activity 8

Write a letter to a friend telling him/her about the things that have changed in your life over the last year.

6. Past Continuous – Used To – Was Going To

Past Continuous: was / were + verb -ing

Affirmative	Interrogative	Negative	
		Long form	**Short form**
I was helping	Was I helping?	I was not helping	I wasn't helping
You were helping	Were you helping?	You were not helping	You weren't helping
He was helping	Was he helping?	He was not helping	He wasn't helping etc.
She was helping	Was she helping?	She was not helping	
It was helping	Was it helping?	It was not helping	**Negative - Interrogative**
We were helping	Were we helping?	We were not helping	
You were helping	Were you helping?	You were not helping	Wasn't I helping?
They were helping	Were they helping?	They were not helping	Weren't you helping? etc.

Time words used with the Past Continuous: while   when   as

Past Continuous versus Past Simple

Past Continuous is used:

1. for an action that was **in the middle of happening** at a stated time in the past.

   At 8 o'clock last night she **was watching** TV.

Past Simple is used:

1. for an action **completed** at a stated time in the past.

   He **finished** his homework at 7 o'clock.

6. Past Continuous - Used To - Was Going To

2. for two or more actions which were happening at the same time in the past (simultaneous actions).

They **were dancing** while he **was playing** the guitar.

3. for a past action which was in progress when another action interrupted it. We use Past Continuous for the interrupted action and Past Simple for the action which interrupts it.

He **was painting** the bedroom when suddenly he **fell off** the ladder.

4. to describe the background to the events in a story.
We **were walking** in the woods. It **was raining** hard...

2. for actions which happened one after another (sequence of actions).

He **slipped**, **fell over** and **broke** his ankle.

3. with non-continuous verbs: appear (= seem), believe, belong, cost, feel, forget, hate, have (= possess), know, like, love, mean, need, prefer, realise, remember, see, seem, smell, sound, suppose, taste, think, understand, want etc.

He **wanted** to buy a new sports car but he couldn't afford one.

4. for past actions which won't happen again.
Shakespeare **wrote** a lot of plays.
(Shakespeare is dead. He won't write any more.)

78 Identify the speech situations, then write sentences as in the example:

action in the middle, simultaneous actions, sequence of actions, completed action, interrupted action, non-continuous verb, action which won't happen again

1. *action in the middle* ....   2. ....   3. ....

(at 11 o'clock / sleep) *They were sleeping at 11 o'clock.*

(wash up/feed the dog/an hour ago)

(last night/knit/watch TV)

6. Past Continuous - Used To - Was Going To

4. ....
(sunbathe/rain)

5. ....
(build/the Eiffel Tower)

6. ....
(have a party/last night)

7. ....
(cook/yesterday/burn her finger)

8. ....
(laugh/cry yesterday morning)

9. ....
(chicken/taste/awful/yesterday)

Was / Were Going To

Was going to is used to express fixed arrangements in the past, unfulfilled plans or an action which someone intended to do in the past but didn't do.

He got up early. **He was going to** catch the 6 o'clock train. (fixed arrangement in the past)
She was going to travel around Europe but she didn't because she fell ill. (unfulfilled plan)
She was going to buy a new car but in the end she repaired her old one.
(She intended to buy a car but she didn't.)

(79) Write what was going to happen but didn't.

1. *She was going to buy a dress* but a thief stole her bag.

2. .... but he was too late.

3. .... but it blew up.

6. Past Continuous - Used To - Was Going To

80 Using the notes first talk about the picture, then write a paragraph.

Mary and George - dance - while music - play loud. Bob and Ben - drink Coke - while Kristi - eat sandwiches. Ted and Steve - sing. Alison - clean - while dog bark. James - sleep on the sofa - while Sheila - try - wake him up. Edward and Lucy - laugh. Susan - bring coffee. Chris - leave the party - while Paula - cry - because not want - him to leave.

They were having a party when the doorbell rang. Peter opened the door and an angry policeman entered the room. Mary and George were dancing while ....
....
....
....
....
....
....
....

Used To

Used to is used to talk about **past habits**. It has the same form in all persons, singular and plural. It forms its negative and interrogative form with **did**.

I used to cry when I was a baby.   **I didn't use to** sleep late.   **Did you use to** sleep late?

81 Look at the pictures and write what Helen used or didn't use to be or have.

Then   Now   Then   Now   Then   Now

1. Helen used to be .... fat.   2. .... short hair.   3. .... a cat.
She didn't use to be thin.
She is thin now. ....

45

6. Past Continuous - Used To - Was Going To

82 First say and then write what you used or didn't use to do when you were five.

....
....
....

83 Put the verbs in brackets into Past Continuous or Past Simple.

Last night I 1) ..had.. (have) a wonderful dream. This is what I 2) .... (dream). We 3) .... (take) a trip to Hawaii. I 4) .... (be) with my family and two of my friends. We 5) .... (be) on a ship and we 6) .... (travel) to Honolulu. On the ship there 7) .... (be) a disco. We 8) .... (sit) on nice comfortable seats and we 9) .... (drink) exotic juices. Lots of people 10) .... (dance) and the music 11) .... (play) loudly. We 12) .... (have) a lot of fun! When the ship 13) .... (arrive) in Honolulu a man 14) .... (wait) to take us to our hotel. The hotel where we 15) .... (stay) was by a beach lined with palm trees. Drums 16) .... (beat) and people on the beach 17) .... (sing) and 18) .... (dance) to the music. The music 19) .... (get) louder and louder until I 20) .... (can) hear a ringing in my ears. It 21) .... (be) my alarm clock! It 22) .... (be) 7 o'clock and time to get up for school.

84 Put the verbs in brackets into Past Simple or Past Continuous.

Dear Peter,
I'm writing to tell you about what happened to me last week while I 1) ..was visiting.. (visit) my aunt who lives by the sea. One afternoon I 2) .... (take) her dog for a walk by the cliffs when I 3) .... (notice) a girl who 4) .... (climb) a tree by the edge of the cliff. As she 5) .... (hang) there, the branch suddenly 6) .... (break) and the girl 7) .... (fall) over the edge. I 8) .... (run) to the edge, but although the girl 9) .... (shout) for help, I 10) .... (not/be able to) see her. I 11) .... (think) about what to do when a man 12) .... (come) along the cliff path. I 13) .... (explain) what had happened and while he 14) .... (go) for help I 15) .... (talk) to the girl. Well, everything 16) .... (end) happily. The girl was rescued and her parents 17) .... (thank) me by giving me a large bunch of flowers. The story 18) .... (be) in the newspaper too! That's all my news - write and tell me yours soon.

With love,
Lucy

6. Past Continuous - Used To - Was Going To

85 Match the sentences, then join them using when, while or and.

PART A
1. John was listening to the radio
2. Peter was swimming
3. He fell over
4. The robbers stole the car
5. Helen was writing a letter

PART B
A. they drove away.
B. the batteries ran out.
C. his sister was sunbathing.
D. her pen broke.
E. he was crossing the road.

1. ...B (when)......
2. ....
3. ....
4. ....
5. ....

86 Choose a verb from the list and complete the text using Past S. or Past Cont.

be, drive, shine, stop, look, seem, hear, fly, can, feel, wonder, go, think, get into, talk

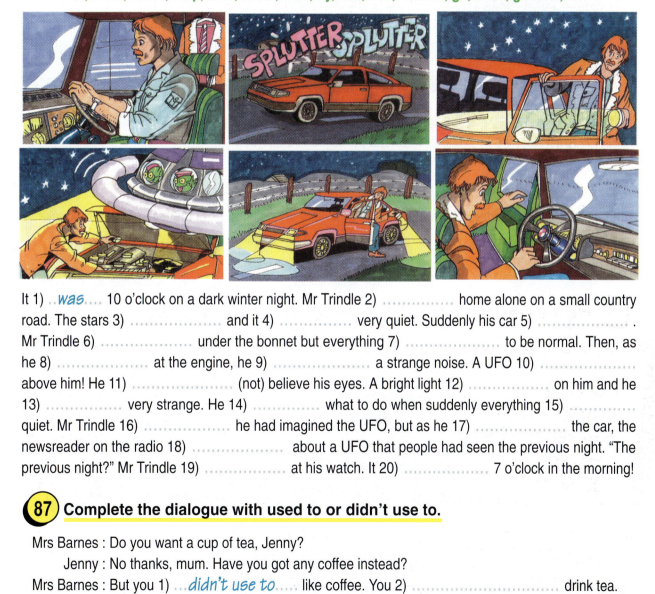

It 1) ...was... 10 o'clock on a dark winter night. Mr Trindle 2) .... home alone on a small country road. The stars 3) .... and it 4) .... very quiet. Suddenly his car 5) .... Mr Trindle 6) .... under the bonnet but everything 7) .... to be normal. Then, as he 8) .... at the engine, he 9) .... a strange noise. A UFO 10) .... above him! He 11) .... (not) believe his eyes. A bright light 12) .... on him and he 13) .... very strange. He 14) .... what to do when suddenly everything 15) .... quiet. Mr Trindle 16) .... he had imagined the UFO, but as he 17) .... the car, the newsreader on the radio 18) .... about a UFO that people had seen the previous night. "The previous night?" Mr Trindle 19) .... at his watch. It 20) .... 7 o'clock in the morning!

87 Complete the dialogue with used to or didn't use to.

Mrs Barnes : Do you want a cup of tea, Jenny?
Jenny : No thanks, mum. Have you got any coffee instead?
Mrs Barnes : But you 1) ...didn't use to... like coffee. You 2) .... drink tea.
Jenny : Yes, but I like it now. Could you put some sugar in it?
Mrs Barnes : You 3) .... take sugar. You 4) .... say it would make you put on weight. Do you want some cornflakes?

6. Past Continuous - Used To - Was Going To

Jenny : Haven't you got any croissants? I 5) .... like cornflakes but I don't now.
Mrs Barnes : You 6) .... be so fussy before you went to Paris.

88) Put the verbs into Past Cont., Past S., was / were going to or used to form.

Policeman : What 1) ...*were you doing*........ (you / do) at 9 o'clock last night?
Witness : I 2) .... (watch) TV while my wife 3) .... (make) dinner. We 4) .... (have) dinner at a restaurant but we 5) .... (not / have) enough money. We 6) .... (go) out a lot but we can't afford to now.
Policeman : What 7) .... (happen) then?
Witness : I 8) .... (think) I 9) .... (hear) a gunshot from outside. I 10) .... (go) outside but I 11) .... (not/see) anything unusual. Then I 12) .... (realise) what the noise was. Our neighbours 13) .... (have) a party and they 14) .... (set off) fireworks in their garden. It 15) .... (not/be) a gunshot after all, officer.

Oral Activity 11 (Question and answer game)

In two teams students cover the text for Ex. 80 then by looking at the picture ask and answer questions.
eg. Was Kristi sleeping on the sofa when the policeman came? etc.

Oral Activity 12

Look at the picture and the list of words to say what they were doing/did at the time of the earthquake.

sleep - wake up - cry   cook - drop the saucepan   play - stand up - run
carry - spill coffee   wash - come out   sit - fall off

Writing Activity 9

Write a letter to your penfriend in Germany to tell him/her what was happening or happened at the time of an earthquake. (60-80 words) *eg. Dear Hans, two days ago there was a terrible earthquake here. It was such a nasty experience. At the time of the earthquake the baby was sleeping. He woke up and started crying...*

7. Reflexive – Emphatic Pronouns & Possessives

Does **your** dog bite?
Oh no! I trained it **myself** not to bite.

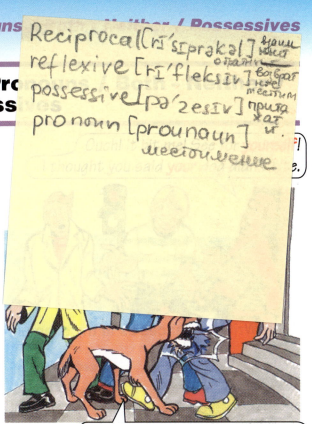

But that dog isn't **mine**! It's **his**.

(handwritten note:)
Reciprocal [rɪˈsɪprəkəl] взаим. отнош.
reflexive [rɪˈfleksɪv] возвр.
possessive [pəˈzesɪv] притяж.
pronoun [prounaun] местоимение

Reflexive-Emphatic pronouns	Personal pronouns		Possessive adjectives	Possessive pronouns
	before verbs as subjects	after verbs as objects	followed by nouns	not followed by nouns
myself	I	me	my	mine
yourself	you	you	your	yours
himself	he	him	his	his
herself	she	her	her	hers
itself	it	it	its	---
ourselves	we	us	our	ours
yourselves	you	you	your	yours
themselves	they	them	their	theirs

Reflexive Pronouns are used :

after certain verbs (**kill**, **cut**, **behave**, **burn**, **enjoy**, **hurt**, **look at**, **teach** etc) when the subject and the object of the verb are the same person. I've cut **myself**.

Emphatic Pronouns are used :

at the end of the sentence or after the noun phrase they refer to, to emphasize the noun or the fact that **one person** and not another performs an action. **He** can fix the car (by) **himself**.

Note these expressions :   **Enjoy yourself!** = Have a good time!   **Behave yourself!** = Be good!
I like being by myself. = I like being alone.   **She lives by herself.** = She lives alone.   **Help yourself to tea!** = Don't wait to be offered tea!

7. Reflexive - Emphatic Pronouns / Both - Neither / Possessives

Note the difference : - **selves** / **each other**

Some old people talk to **themselves**.

They are talking to **each other**.

89 Write sentences as in the example :

1. What is she doing? She *is looking* (look) at *herself* in the mirror.

2. What has he done? He *cut himself* (cut) .... with a knife.

3. What are they doing? They *are enjoying* (enjoy) *themselves* at a party.

4. "What have you done?" "We *'ve hurt* (hurt) *ourselves*."

5. What has she done? She *has burnt* (burn) *herself* on the cooker.

6. "What are you doing?" "I *'m drying* (dry) *myself* with my towel."

7. Reflexive - Emphatic Pronouns / Both - Neither / Possessives

90 Fill in : myself, yourself, himself, ourselves or yourselves.

Jim : Bye Mum. We're going to Simon's birthday party.
Mum : O.K. Enjoy 1) ...*yourselves*... boys. And Jim, don't eat too much cake or you'll make 2) ...*yourself*... sick. Have you got a card to take with you?
Jim : Yes, we have. Mark and I made it 3) ...*ourselves*... . What are you and Dad going to do this afternoon, Mum?
Mum : I'm going to buy 4) ...*myself*... some new clothes and Dad's going to study. He's trying to teach 5) ...*himself*... Italian. Have a good time at the party, but behave 6) ...*yourselves*... .

91 Fill in the appropriate reflexive or emphatic pronouns.

1. My dad cut ...*himself*... shaving yesterday.
2. Julie cooked ...*herself*... some dinner.
3. Please, help ...*yourself*... to more biscuits, John!
4. I enjoyed ...*myself*... at the party last night.
5. We don't need any help. We can do it ...*ourselves*... .
6. The children drew all these pictures ...*themselves*... .

92 Fill in the appropriate reflexive pronouns.

Yesterday my sister and I went to the shop to buy 1) ...*ourselves*... some chocolate. On the way home, Tonia fell down and hurt 2) ...*herself*... and I cut 3) ...*myself*... on some broken glass. When we got home, my brother and his friends were enjoying 4) ...*themselves*... playing in the garden. My brother shouted, "Look at 5) ...*yourselves*..." and he began to laugh at us. When we looked at 6) ...*ourselves*... in the mirror, there was nothing wrong except for some chocolate round our mouths.

Possessive case with 's / s'	Possessive case with "of"
1. **singular nouns + 's** (person or animal) the boy**'s** bag, the cat**'s** head	1. **of** + name of a thing the banks **of** the river
2. **regular plural nouns + '** the boy**s'** bags	2. **of** + possessive case/possessive pronoun That's a friend **of Mary's** (= one of Mary's friends). I've got a book **of yours** (= one of your books).
3. **irregular plural nouns not ending in s/-es + 's** the children**'s** toys	

Note: **phrase of place + 's** : at the chemist**'s** = at the chemist's shop

phrase of time + 's / ' : today**'s** paper = the paper that has come out today

two week**s'** holiday = a holiday that lasts for two weeks

7. Reflexive - Emphatic Pronouns / Both - Neither / Possessives

93 Write as in the example :

Julie — car
1. This is Julie's car.
   It's her car.
   It's hers.

the girls — house
2. ....

John — records
3. ....

women — shoes
4. ....

94 Fill in the correct subject/object/possessive pronouns or adjectives.

Last year Francis and 1) ....his.... sister Caroline went on holiday to Paris. Unfortunately, 2) .... was a disaster. First of all, 3) .... nearly missed 4) .... flight because 5) .... car broke down. Then Francis couldn't find 6) .... ticket, until Caroline realised that she had both 7) .... ticket and 8) .... in 9) .... handbag. When 10) .... got to Paris, 11) .... couldn't find 12) .... hotel. Caroline fell over and twisted 13) .... ankle when 14) .... climbed out of the taxi. Francis tried to help 15) .... and strained 16) .... back, so 17) .... both had to spend the rest of the week in bed. This year 18) .... are hoping to see some of the sights of Paris on 19) .... holiday.

95 Underline the correct item.

1. She's got a pen of (you / <u>yours</u>).
2. These are (the boys' shirts / shirts of the boys).
3. He is a friend of (my / mine).
4. We're having (two days' holiday / a holiday of two days).
5. She went to the (baker shop / baker's).
6. That's the (house's kitchen / kitchen of the house).

7. Reflexive - Emphatic Pronouns / Both - Neither / Possessives

	Positive some	Interrogative any	Negative no/not any
people	someone somebody	anyone anybody	no one / not anyone nobody / not anybody
things	something	anything	nothing / not anything
place	somewhere	anywhere	nowhere / not anywhere

96 Fill in: some, any, no or their derivatives.

When the three bears came home, the mother bear said, "1) ...*Some*... of the soup has gone!" The little bear looked in his bowl and said, "There is 2) .... soup in my bowl! There isn't 3) .... left at all! 4) .... has eaten it!" Then the bears heard 5) .... in the bedroom. The father bear called, "Is there 6) .... there?" but 7) .... answered. The little girl in the bedroom woke up and looked for 8) .... to hide, but she couldn't find 9) .... The father bear called again, "Is there 10) .... there?" and the frightened girl said, "No, there's 11) .... here at all!"

Both - Neither - None - All

Both refers to **two** people or things. It has a **positive meaning** and takes a verb in the **plural**.
Tom is rich. Laura is rich too.
Both of them **are** rich. **or** They are **both** rich.

Neither refers to **two** people or things. It has a **negative meaning** and takes a verb either in the **singular** or the **plural**.
Tom isn't poor. Laura isn't poor either.
Neither of them **is / are** poor.

All refers to **more than two** people or things. It has a **positive meaning** and takes a verb in the **plural**.
John, Mary and Kevin are students. **All of** them **are** students. **or** They are **all** students.

None refers to **more than two** people or things. It has a **negative meaning** and takes a verb either in the **singular** or the **plural**.
John, Mary and Kevin haven't got a car.
None of them **has / have** a car.

97 Use both, neither, none or all and write sentences as in the example :

1. Kate can ride a bicycle. Sue can ride a bicycle too.
Both of them can ride a bicycle. **or** *They can both ride a bicycle.*

2. John doesn't like fish. Greg doesn't like fish either.
....
....
....

7. Reflexive - Emphatic Pronouns / Both - Neither / Possessives

3. Mr Tibbs doesn't drive carefully. Mr Smith doesn't drive carefully either.
....
....

4. Lyn, Sally and Moira are swimming.
....
....
....
....

5. Ted has eaten a pizza. Tony has eaten a pizza too.
....
....
....

6. Ann hasn't typed any letters today. Nina hasn't typed any letters today either.
....
....

7. Bob, Nick and Ted don't speak French.
....
....

8. Helen, Jane and Sue like ice-cream.
....
....

98) Write sentences using the correct pronouns.

1. John / first day at work / enjoy / boss / given / nice office.
   It's John's first day at work. He's enjoying himself. The boss has given him a nice office.
2. Tracy / first day at school / enjoy / teacher / just given / jigsaw puzzle.
   ....
3. we / first day at university / enjoy / professor / just given / interesting talk.
   ....
4. I / first day on holiday / enjoy / hotel clerk / just given / key to room.
   ....
5. the Smiths / first day in new house / enjoy / friends / just given / present.
   ....

Oral Activity 13

The teacher divides the class into two teams and says a subject pronoun. The teams in turn must say the possessive adjectives and possessive and reflexive pronouns which correspond to the subject pronoun. Each correct answer gets 1 point. The team with the most points is the winner.

Teacher :	I
Team A S1 :	my, mine, myself
Teacher :	You (plural)
Team B S1 :	your, yours, yourselves

Teacher :	he
Team A S2 :	his, his, hiself
Teacher :	No. Not hiself, but himself. Team A doesn't get a point.

7. Reflexive - Emphatic Pronouns / Both - Neither / Possessives

99 Look at the family tree and talk about it.

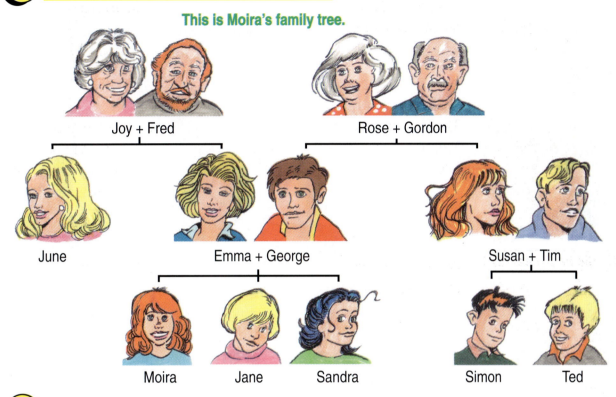

100 Look at the above family tree and fill in the correct pronouns and possessives.

Fred is Joy's husband. 1) ...*He*... is 2) .... husband. Joy is June and Emma's mother. 3) .... is 4) .... mother. Emma is George's wife. 5) .... is 6) .... wife. Moira is Emma and George's daughter. 7) .... is 8) .... daughter. Jane and Sandra are Moira's sisters. 9) .... are 10) .... sisters. June is Moira, Jane and Sandra's aunt. 11) .... is 12) .... aunt. Simon is Moira's cousin. 13) .... is 14) .... cousin. Susan and Tim are Simon and Ted's parents. 15) .... are 16) .... parents. Susan's parents are Rose and Gordon. 17) .... are 18) .... parents. All these people are Moira's family. 19) .... are 20) .... family.

Oral Activity 14

Using **both** or **all**, say what the following groups of words have in common.

1. oranges, apples, pears
2. Prince, Michael Jackson
3. football, basketball
4. London, Paris, Athens
5. Italy, Germany
6. green, red, brown
7. January, February
8. horses, cows, dogs
9. BMW, Golf
10. baker's, butcher's, grocer's

eg. 1. ....*They are all fruit.*......   or   .....*All of them are fruit.*......

Writing Activity 10

Using Ex. 100 as a model, write about your family tree. Then introduce your family to your partner.

8. Past Perfect – Past Perfect Continuous

Past Perfect: had + past participle

Affirmative		Negative		Interrogative
Long form	**Short form**	**Long form**	**Short form**	
I had waited	I'd waited	I had not waited	I hadn't waited	Had I waited?
You had waited	You'd waited	You had not waited	You hadn't waited	Had you waited?
He had waited	He'd waited	He had not waited	He hadn't waited	Had he waited?
She had waited	She'd waited	She had not waited	She hadn't waited	Had she waited? etc
It had waited	It'd waited	It had not waited	It hadn't waited	**Negative-Interrogative**
We had waited	We'd waited	We had not waited	We hadn't waited	Hadn't you waited?
You had waited	You'd waited	You had not waited	You hadn't waited	Hadn't he waited? etc
They had waited	They'd waited	They had not waited	They hadn't waited	

Past Perfect Continuous: had been + verb -ing

Affirmative	Negative	Interrogative
I had been waiting	I had not been waiting	Had I been waiting?
You had been waiting	You had not been waiting	Had you been waiting?
He had been waiting	He had not been waiting	Had he been waiting?
She had been waiting	She had not been waiting	Had she been waiting?
It had been waiting	It had not been waiting	Had it been waiting?
We had been waiting	We had not been waiting	Had we been waiting?
You had been waiting	You had not been waiting	Had you been waiting?
They had been waiting	They had not been waiting	Had they been waiting?
Short form	**Short form**	**Negative-Interrogative**
I'd been waiting ... etc	I hadn't been waiting ... etc	Hadn't you been waiting? etc

8. Past Perfect - Past Perfect Continuous

Time expressions used with Past Perfect and Past Perfect Continuous:

before, after, just, yet, already, for, since, ever, never, till/until, when, by, by the time etc

Past Perfect Simple is used:	**Past Perfect Continuous is used:**
for a past action which happened **before** another **past action** or **before** a stated **past time**. She **had already left** when I got home. She **had arrived** by 8 o'clock	for an action continuing up to a specific time in the past. He **had been waiting for an hour** before she arrived.
for a complete action.	for a continuous, past action which had visible results or effect in the past.

She **had cleaned** the house by 6 o'clock.

She was tired. She **had been cleaning** the house all morning.

as the past equivalent of Present Perfect. (see p. 38)
She **isn't** in her office. She **has already left**.
(before a present time)
She **wasn't** in her office. She **had already left**.
(before a past time)

as the past equivalent of Present Perfect Continuous. (see p. 38)
She **is** tired. She **has been working** hard all morning. (present time)
She **was** tired. She **had been working** hard all morning. (past time)

101 Fill in the Present Perfect S. or Cont. or Past Perfect S. or Cont.

1. Her feet ached last Monday. She ...*had been walking*... (walk) for six hours.

2. Don is cold. He ....(swim) in the lake.

3. He can't pay the bill. He .... (lose) his wallet.

8. Past Perfect - Past Perfect Continuous

4. The woman drowned in the river. She .... (swim).

5. He bought a car after he .... (save) enough money.

6. She signed the letter after she .... (write) it.

7. Her hair is wet. She .... (wash) it.

8. He felt sick because he .... (eat) too much.

9. He was hot. He .... (run) for an hour.

Short answers

| **Had** I/you/he/she/it/we/you/they eaten lunch? | Yes, I/you/he/she/it/we/you/they **had**. | No, I/you/he/she/it/we/you/they **hadn't**. |

102 Look at the picture, ask and answer questions as in the example:

It's the day after Christmas. Last night the Dicksons had a party at their house. What had they done and what hadn't they done before they went to bed?

1. (they / open / all presents) ...*Had they opened all the presents? Yes, they had.*...........

2. (they / drink / lemonade) ....

3. (they / eat / all the cake) ....

4. (they / let / cat in) ....

5. (they / eat / turkey) ....

6. (they / tidy / the room) ....

8. Past Perfect - Past Perfect Continuous

103 Fill in Past Simple or Past Perfect, then state which action happened first.

1. When I ..*arrived*.. (arrive) at the station, the train ..*had left*.. (leave). **first action** : ..*had left*....
2. We .... (light) the candles because the lights .... (go off).
   first action : ....
3. When I got home I .... (discover) that somebody .... (break into) my flat.
   first action : ....
4. The patient .... (die) before the ambulance .... (reach) the hospital.
   first action : ....
5. John .... (eat) all the cakes by the time the other children .... (arrive) at the party. **first action** : ....

104 Write what each person had been doing using verbs from the list below.

sleep, write, walk, wash, play, cut, listen, work

1. Jane's clothes were wet.
   She ..*had been washing*.......... her dog.
2. The boys were dirty.
   They .... football.
3. John was not happy that the noise woke him.
   He ....
4. Dave had stains on his shoes.
   He .... the grass.
5. Carol's ears hurt.
   She .... to the radio for two hours.
6. Kate had black ink on her hands.
   She .... for three hours.
7. Anne's feet hurt.
   She .... for two hours.
8. Nina looked tired.
   She .... all morning.

Note the difference :

Past Perfect

When Tom phoned he **had left**.
(He left before Tom phoned.)

Past Simple

When she phoned he **left**.
(She phoned and then he left.)

Past Perfect Continuous

When she arrived they **had been fighting**.
(She arrived after the fight.)

Past Continuous

When she arrived they **were fighting**.
(When she arrived they were in the middle of the fight.)

8. Past Perfect - Past Perfect Continuous

105 Put the verbs in brackets into Past Perfect or Past Simple.

1. John ...*lit*... (light) the candles when she arrived.

2. George .... (light) the candles when she arrived.

3. When she arrived at the theatre he .... (buy) the tickets.

4. When she arrived at the theatre he .... (buy) the tickets.

5. When he came home she .... (have) dinner with him.

6. When he came home she .... (already/have) dinner.

106 Write the situations (action up to a past time or interrupted action), then put the verbs into Past Perfect Continuous or Past Continuous.

1. ...*action up to a past time*...

Her eyes were red. She ....*had been crying*.... (cry).

2. ....

She .... (cry) when he came in.

3. ....

She .... (type) a letter when the fire started.

4. ....

She looked tired. She .... (type) letters all morning.

5. ....

He hit his head. He .... (play) football.

6. ....

He .... (play) football when the ball hit his head.

8. Past Perfect - Past Perfect Continuous

107 Put the verbs in brackets into Past Perfect or Past Perfect Continuous.

Mr Thomas was exhausted. He 1) ...had had..... (have) the worst morning of his life! Everything 2) .... (go) wrong. He 3) .... (drive) to work for half an hour when suddenly his car broke down. Not wanting to be late he decided to start walking and try to catch a bus. After he 4) .... (walk) for over an hour, it began to rain. However, just at that moment a taxi appeared and Mr Thomas jumped in. When he arrived at the office, he realised that he 5) .... (leave) his wallet in his own car and he had no money to pay the driver! He rushed into the office, followed by the angry taxi driver. However, an important business meeting 6) .... (just/start). Mr Thomas was wet and dirty because it 7) .... (rain) and his boss was very angry because he 8) .... (wait) for him to arrive for over an hour. After explaining what 9) .... (happen) to his boss, Mr Thomas borrowed a car and went home to change. When he arrived home he realised to his horror that someone 10) .... (break into) his house. What a morning!

108 Put the verbs in brackets into Past Perfect or Past Simple.

After Jim and Terry 1) ...had finished.... (finish) their breakfast, they 2) .... (take) their bags and 3) .... (go) to the river to fish. They 4) .... (go) there before and 5) .... (catch) some big fish. By 5 o' clock they 6) .... (not/get) any fish, so they decided to go home. They 7) .... (promise) their mother to bring fish for dinner, so they 8) .... (look) for a shop where they could buy some but the shops 9) .... (already/close). When they 10) .... (arrive) home, they 11) .... (tell) their mother that they 12) .... (catch) the biggest fish they 13) .... (ever/see) but it 14) .... (escape).

109 Put the verbs in brackets into the correct tense.

1. Tony ..bought............ (buy) a new shirt last Monday.
2. Ann is a teacher. She .... (teach) for fifteen years.
3. She .... (cook) lunch before the children came home.
4. How long .... (you / have) a driving licence?
5. She .... (type) some letters when the boss asked her into his office.
6. He .... (drive) for an hour when he reached the village.

8. Past Perfect - Past Perfect Continuous

110 Put the verbs in brackets into the correct tense.

"A lion 1) ..has escaped... (escape) from London Zoo. The zoo-keeper 2) .... (clean) the lion's cage when suddenly a lion 3) .... (bite) him and 4) .... (run) out of the cage. The zoo-keeper 5) .... (recover) in hospital now. When he 6) .... (arrive) at the hospital he 7) .... (lose) a lot of blood, but the doctors 8) .... (think) he will be alright. Lots of people 9) .... (see) the lion already. The police 10) .... (stop) a summer carnival which London Zoo 11) .... (plan) and at present they 12) .... (hunt) for the lion. They 13) .... (advise) us to tell the public to stay indoors until they 14) .... (catch) the lion."

Oral Activity 15

The teacher divides the class into two teams and asks students in turn to give reasons why they were pleased the last time something nice happened. Each correct sentence gets 1 point. The team with the most points is the winner.

  Team A S1: The last time I was pleased was because I had received a present.
  Team B S1: The last time I was pleased was because I had passed a test.
  Team A S2: The last time I was pleased was because I had won a prize. etc.

Oral Activity 16

The teacher divides the class into two teams and asks students to look at the following situations, giving reasons in turn for each situation. Each correct reason gets 1 point. The team with the most points is the winner.

  1. Ben couldn't write the letter because ... *he had lost his pen.* ....
  2. Jane missed the train because ....
  3. He couldn't pay the electricity bill because ....
  4. She failed her exam because ....
  5. She was sad because ....
  6. His hands were dirty because ....
  7. He was wet because ....
  8. They were hungry because ....since morning.
  9. He had a stomach-ache because ....
  10. They were tired because ....
  11. He had a black eye because ....
  12. Jennifer got sunburnt because ....for over five hours.

Revision Exercises II

Writing Activity 11

Last Monday you had an argument with your best friend. However, later you realised that the argument was all your fault. Write a letter of apology explaining why you behaved in such a way. (60-80 words).
Dear Tony,
  I'm writing to say I'm sorry we argued last Monday, but I had had lots of problems that day.

 Revision Exercises II

111 Choose the correct item.

1. "Have you ever ..B.. Helsinki?" "Yes, once, in 1989."
   A) gone to   B) been to   C) been in
2. She is the .... student in the class.
   A) clever   B) cleverest   C) more clever
3. While she was chopping onions she accidentally cut ....
   A) herself   B) himself   C) her
4. .... your invitation to the wedding yet?
   A) Hadn't you got   B) Haven't you got
   C) Didn't you get
5. He .... live in London, but now he lives in a village.
   A) uses   B) used to   C) was used to
6. She .... in this house for 25 years.
   A) has lived   B) lives   C) is living
7. John! .... wants you on the phone.
   A) Some   B) Something   C) Someone
8. She .... French before she became a teacher.
   A) had studied   B) has studied
   C) has been studying

112 Find the mistake and correct it.

1. You are out of breath. Were you running? .... *Have you been* ....
2. She is already in Istanbul for a week. ....
3. Jane runs fastest than Margaret. ....
4. He helped herself to a piece of cake. ....
5. They live anywhere near the bus station. ....
6. He looked angry. Has he been arguing? ....
7. Where have you been? I have waited for 45 minutes! ....
8. He cleans the house at the moment. ....
9. She has written three books before she became famous. ....
10. He speaks so quick that I can't understand him. ....

113 Put the verbs in brackets into Present Simple, Present Continuous or Future.

Paul: Hello, David. How 1) .... *are you* ...... (you/be)?
David: I 2) .... (be) fine. I 3) .... (watch) a programme on TV. It 4) .... (not/be) very good but there 5) .... (be) nothing else on.

Revision Exercises II

Paul: 6) .... (you/want) to come to the cinema this evening? I 7) .... (see) a film at the Rex.
David: I really have to study, but 8) .... (I/ask) Tom if he wants to go?
Paul: That's a good idea. I 9) .... (wait).

114 Put the words in the correct order to make sentences.

1. She left/suddenly/ at 6 o'clock/ the room
   ...*She left the room suddenly at 6 o'clock.*...
2. They've bought a /two-storey/lovely/in London/old-fashioned/house
   ....
3. He walked/in the rain/up the hill/slowly
   ....
4. Every Monday/to the gym/by car/they go
   ....
5. He's built a/wooden/beautiful/bookcase
   ....
6. She was wearing a(n)/white/elegant/long/wedding/dress
   ....

115 Underline the correct item.

1. That cake looks <u>wonderful</u>/wonderfully.
2. This salad tastes terrible/terribly. What have you put in it?
3. He draws very good/well but he can't paint at all.
4. Have you got a cold? Your voice sounds unusual/unusually.
5. She ran up the stairs as quick/quickly as she could.
6. When he woke up he still felt sleepy/sleepily.
7. She spoke very rude/rudely to me.
8. This game seems easy/easily, but it isn't really.
9. That music sounds very strange/strangely from here.
10. If you work hard/hardly, you will certainly succeed.

Note that the verbs sound, look, taste, feel, seem are followed by an adjective.

116 Put the verbs into Past S., Past Cont., Present Perfect or Present Perfect Cont.

When John Mills 1) ..*was*.. (be) eighteen he 2) .... (leave) his home in the country and 3) .... (go) to study in London. While he 4) .... (study) at the University there, someone 5) .... (offer) him a job as a salesperson. At that time he 6) .... (try) to finish his degree so he 7) .... (turn down) the job. Since then he 8) .... (do) many kinds of jobs, including teaching and farming. He 9) .... (also/run) a shop, which is the only job he 10) .... (not/like). Since last September he 11) .... (try) to find a job in an art gallery because he wants to learn about paintings, but so far he 12) .... (not/have) much luck.

Revision Exercises II

117 **Fill in the correct reflexive pronouns.**

When Jane woke up on Monday, she saw the note she had written to 1) ...*herself*... so she would remember to visit her boss in the hospital. He'd fallen off a ladder and hurt 2) .... quite badly. She knew her children could dress and feed 3) ...., so she got dressed and left immediately. She drove to the hospital, got out of the car and shut the door. Then she saw the keys inside. "Oh no, I've locked 4) .... out!" she said to 5) .... She knew it was the start of a terrible day.

118 **Fill in the blanks as in the example :**

Dear Susan,
Well, we've moved into the new house at last! It was a lot of work, but everything is so much 1) ..*better*.. (good) here that it was worth it. There are not many rooms but they are 2) .... (big) I've ever seen in a house of this size. The neighbourhood is a lot 3) .... (quiet) than our old one, and the people here are 4) .... (friendly). The garden is 6) .... (nice) I've (helpful) and much 5) .... ever had - it's a real pleasure to work in! All in all, I think this is 7) .... (good) house we've ever lived in. You must come and visit us soon.
Love,
Diana

119 **Fill in: Present Perfect, Present Perfect Cont., Past Perfect or Past Perfect Cont.**

Dear Jerry,
I'm sorry I 1) ..*haven't written*.. (not/write) for a long time but I 2) .... (work) very hard lately so I 3) .... (not/have) much time for other things. I 4) .... (plan) to come up to Scotland for a visit next month, but what I 5) .... (not/realise) was that my partner 6) .... (already/plan) to go on holiday at the same time, so mine will have to wait. What 7) .... (Mary/find) a new job? I was surprised to hear (you/do) lately? 8) .... that she 9) .... (lose) her job after she 10) .... (do) so well there. Write soon and tell me your news.
Yours,
Bob

Revision Exercises II

120 Put the verbs in brackets into the correct tense.

1. I ...*have already seen*.... (already/see) that film twice, but I'd like to see it again.
2. How long ago .... (you / move) to this house?
3. Yesterday afternoon it .... (still / rain) when I got home.
4. Tony .... (act) for many years before he became famous.
5. The students .... (write) for two hours when the teacher told them to stop.
6. I .... (wait) for more than two hours. Where .... (you /be)?
7. It .... (probably / snow) tomorrow.
8. He .... (lock) all the windows before he left home.
9. She .... (do) the cleaning by 6 o'clock yesterday.
10. He .... (clean) the car when the phone rang, so he didn't answer it.
11. "How long .... (you / work) for this company?" "For ten years and I like it here."

121 Look at the table and answer the questions.

	Tom, 19	**Dick, 18**	**Harry, 21**
Lives in	London	Birmingham	Sheffield
Studies	Maths	Law	Medicine
Sports	cricket	football	tennis
Enjoys	chess, walking	cinema	playing guitar, walking
Family	1 sister	2 brothers, 1 sister	1 sister
Ambitions	become a teacher	become a lawyer	become a doctor

1. Who lives in Newcastle? .....*None of them live(s) in Newcastle.*...............
2. Who studies English?
3. Who enjoys walking, Tom or Harry?
4. Who wants to be an artist?
5. Who has straight hair, Tom or Dick?
6. Who is over thirty?
7. Who plays a sport?
8. Who has a sister?
9. Who is wearing glasses, Tom or Harry?
10. Who has a brother, Tom or Harry?
11. Who has got curly hair, Dick or Tom?

9. Functions of Modal Verbs

The modal verbs are: **can**, **could**, **must**, **need**, **will**, **would**, **shall**, **should**, **may**, **might** etc. They have the same form in all persons. They come before the subject in questions and take **not** after them in negations. They take an **infinitive without to** after them.

Can she play tennis? No, she **can't play** tennis but she **can play** golf.

Perhaps I could borrow my neighbour's trumpet.

*But you **can't** play the trumpet.*

*I know, but if I've got it, he **won't be able to** play it either.*

We express ability with:

can (ability in the present or future)	**Can** you swim? No, **I can't**. I **can** run fast though.
could / was able to (ability in the past for repeated actions)	She **could/was able to** dance for hours when she was young. (repeated action)
was able to (= managed to) (ability in the past for repeated actions or a single action)	He **was able to** win the race. (single action)
couldn't / wasn't able to (for repeated or single actions)	I **couldn't/wasn't able to** find my keys. (single action) He **couldn't/wasn't able to** ski when he was young. (repeated action)

Can is the Present Simple form and **could** is the Past Simple. **Can** borrows the rest of its tenses from the verb phrase **be able to**.   eg. She **hasn't been able to** finish it yet.

 Fill in : can, could or be able to in the correct tense.

John : 1) ..*Can*... you ski?
Dave : Yes, I 2) .... I went skiing last year and I 3) .... go down the learner's slope easily.
John : I 4) .... ski when I was younger, but since I hurt my leg I 5) ....
Dave : Actually, I think ice-skating is much easier. I 6) .... ice-skate when I was five years old.
John : Really? I tried ice-skating once, but I 7) .... stand up at all!

9. Functions of Modal Verbs

123 Fill in: can, could, was able to, can't, couldn't or wasn't/haven't been able to.

Dear Mary,
I'm very pleased you 1) **can** come to stay at the weekend. I'm sorry I 2) .... talk to you on the phone yesterday, but I 3) .... leave the baby. I 4) .... get tickets for the theatre on Saturday - I 5) .... wait to go. Mum says that when she was young you 6) .... have a night out for £2! You certainly 7) .... now!
We 8) .... fix the car yet but Mum says we 9) .... borrow hers. By the way, the baby 10) .... say three new words! See you on Friday.
Love, Anna

We express **possibility / probability** with :

may	(= perhaps, very possible)	He **may** be back before noon. (It's possible.)
might	(= perhaps, very possible)	There **might** be some cheese in the fridge. (It's possible.)
could	(= possible)	He **could** still be at home. (It's possible.)
must	(it is almost certain; I think)	They look alike. They **must** be twins. (I think they are twins.)
can't	(it does not seem possible; I don't think)	You have been sleeping all day. You **can't** be tired. (I don't think it's possible that you are tired.)
can he be?	(Is it possible?)	**Can** he still be at work? (Is it possible?)

Although **might** is the past form of **may** it can be used for present situations too. **May** borrows the rest of its tenses from the verb phrase **be allowed to**. eg. He has **not been allowed to** enter the building.

124 Fill in: may, might, could, must or can't.

Dear "Unhappy",
You 1) **can't** be serious about leaving home! There 2) .... be some problems with your family, but there 3) .... be another solution. You 4) .... try talking to a friend or a relative. You 5) .... have some aunts or cousins who can help. You 6) .... find that discussing the problem all together is better. Your parents 7) .... really be as angry as you think; they 8) .... be upset but they 9) .... realise why you're so unhappy. I suggest you try talking to them again – you 10) .... be surprised.

9. Functions of Modal Verbs

125 Fill in : can't, could, may or might.

Sue : How old do you think Steve is?
Mary : He 1) *may* be a bit older than we are, but he certainly 2) .... be more than 25.
Sue : I don't know. He 3) .... be older than you think. He takes very good care of himself, you know. He 4) .... be as old as thirty.
Mary : No, he 5) .... be. I know because he left school just before I did.
Sue : You 6) .... be right, but I'm still not really convinced.

We express permission with :

(asking for permission)

can (informal)	**Can** I borrow your pen?
could (more polite)	**Could** I borrow your car?
may (formal)	**May** I use your phone?
might (more formal)	**Might** I see your driving licence, please?

(giving / refusing permission)

can (informal, giving permission)	You **can** have one more if you want.
may (formal, giving permission)	You **may** stay a little longer.
mustn't (refusing permission)	You **mustn't** park here.
can't (refusing permission)	You **can't** enter this room.

126 Fill in: can, may, could, mustn't or can't.

Jim : Mum, 1) ... *can/may* .. I go to the library?
Mother : Of course you 2) ...., Jim, but you 3) .... stay very long.
Jim : 4) .... I stay until 8 o'clock?
Mother : No, you 5) ...., because the concert starts at 8:30.

(At the library)

Jim : 6) .... I look at the latest "Musician" magazine, please?
Librarian : Yes, you 7) ...., but remember that you 8) .... take it out of the library.

9. Functions of Modal Verbs

We make requests, offers or suggestions with:

can (request)
could (polite request/suggestion)
would you like (polite offer)
Shall I/we (suggestion/offer)

will (offer/request) * for the other uses of "will" (promises, threats etc.) see p. 26

Can you help me tidy my room?
Could I have a little more cake please?
Would you like some more lemonade?
Shall I post this letter for you? (offer)
Shall we buy him a present? (suggestion)
I'll make you some coffee if you want. (friendly offer)
Will you do me a favour? (friendly request)

127 Fill in : can, could, would, shall or will.

John : 1) ...Would... you like some more coffee, darling?
Jane : No, I don't think so. 2) .... we get the bill?
John : OK. Waiter - excuse me, 3) .... you bring us the bill please?
Waiter : Here you are sir. 4) .... I take these plates away?
John : Thank you. 5) .... I have a pen to sign this cheque please? Jane,
  6) .... you give me my glasses?
Waiter : 7) .... you like me to get a taxi for you sir?
John : Yes, please.
Waiter : And I 8) .... bring your coats for you in just a minute.

128 Fill in : can, would, could, shall or will.

Shop Asst : 1) ..Can... I help you?
Customer : Yes, I'm looking for a jumper. 2) .... you show
  me some?
Shop Asst : Yes, of course. What size 3) .... you like?
Customer : Medium, please.
Shop Asst : I 4) .... get some to show you. Is there
  anything else you 5) .... like to see?
Customer : 6) .... I try on some skirts as well?
Shop Asst : Certainly ... ...
Shop Asst : Do you like them?
Customer : Yes, I do. 7) I .... take them all.
Shop Asst : 8) .... I wrap them for you?
Customer : Yes, please.

129 Fill in : will, shall or won't.

Mum : 1) .... Will ...... you be late home tonight, Sally?
Sally : Yes, I 2) .... I'm going to a party. But I 3) .... be too late. I have to work tomorrow.
Mum : 4) .... I keep some dinner hot for you?

9. Functions of Modal Verbs

Sally : No, thanks Mum. There 5) .... be lots to eat at the party.
Mum : 6) .... I come and collect you in the car?
Sally : No, there's no need. I 7) .... come home with Niki.
Mum : Well, 8) .... I wait up until you get back?
Sally : No Mum. Please don't. Oh no! Look at the time! What 9) .... I wear, Mum?

We express advice with :

| should / ought to had better | You **should** walk more. (general advice; I advise you.) You'**d better** see your dentist. (advice for a specific situation; it is a good idea.) |

130 Fill in: should, ought to or had better.

Jill : You 1) ... *should/ought to* ..... ask someone to paint the house this year.
Laura : Yes. It's beginning to look a bit dirty. I can't really afford it, though. Do you think I 2) .... try to get a loan?
Laura : No, you 3) .... not. You might have a problem paying it back.
Jill : I 4) .... do something about the roof as well. It leaks when it rains hard.
Laura : Really? You 5) .... take care of it now or the ceiling will fall in!
Jill : Yes, you're right. I 6) .... ring someone today and ask them to look at it.

We express obligation or necessity with :

| **must** (strong obligation or personal feelings of necessity) **have to** (external necessity) **I've got to** (informal; it's necessary) | We **must** follow the school rules. (obligation; I'm obliged to.) I **must** see a doctor soon. (I decide it is necessary.) I **have to** do my homework every day. (others decide it is necessary) I'**ve got to** leave early today. |

Must is the Present Simple form. It borrows the rest of its tenses from the verb **have to**. To form questions and negations of **have to** we use **do/does** (Pres. S.) and **did** (Past S.).
He **didn't have to** do the shopping yesterday.   You **don't have to** go to school today.
Does he have to be at work on time?

9. Functions of Modal Verbs

131 Fill in: must or have to.

1. I ..must.. water the plants.
2. I .... water the plants.
3. I .... go to bed.
4. I .... go to bed early.
5. I .... be quiet.
6. I .... lose some weight.

We express absence of necessity or prohibition with:

- **mustn't** (prohibition)
- **can't** (prohibition)
- **needn't** (it is not necessary)
- **don't need/have to** (it is not necessary in the present/future)
- **didn't need/have to** (it was not necessary in the past)

You **mustn't** park here. (It's forbidden.)
You **can't** enter the club without a card. (You are not allowed.)
You **needn't** take an umbrella. It isn't raining.
You **don't need/have to** do it now. You can do it later. (It isn't necessary.)
He **didn't need/have to** go to work yesterday because it was Sunday. (It was not necessary.)

132 Fill in: mustn't, needn't, don't need/have to, didn't need/have to, have to or can't.

Mum: You 1) ..can't.. watch TV now. You have to do your homework.

9. Functions of Modal Verbs

Bobby : I 2) .... do it. Doing homework is stupid, anyway.
Dad : Bobby, you 3) .... speak to your mother like that!
Bobby : I'm sorry. Well, at least I 4) .... write a composition today.
Dad : When I was a boy we 5) .... do much homework, but now I'm sorry because I didn't learn much.
Bobby : If you 6) .... do homework, then why 7) .... I .... do mine?

133 Fill in: mustn't, needn't or can't.

John, I want you to look after your brother this evening. He 1) *can't* .. go out and he 2) .... forget to do all his homework. You 3) .... let him watch TV until he's finished it. He 4) .... watch the film either – it starts very late. He 5) .... have a bath; he had one in the morning. There's a cake in the cupboard but you 6) .... eat it all – leave some for your sister. You 7) .... do the washing-up: I'm going to do it tomorrow. You 8) .... make too much noise. We might be quite late home because we 9) .... leave the party tonight until most of the guests have left. And you 10) .... go to bed without having a wash and brushing your teeth. But you 11) .... wait up for us.

134 Make sentences as in the example :

| You | must
mustn't
needn't | touch
buy
take
pull
do
tell | the washing-up. I did it myself.
the cat's tail.
those wires.
your medicine or you won't get better.
me the truth or I'll punish you.
any apples. I bought some yesterday. |

1. *You mustn't touch those wires.* ....
2. ....
3. ....
4. ....
5. ....
6. ....

135 First identify the meaning of the modal verbs, then write a synonym.

(im)possibility - offer - advice - necessity - giving/refusing permission - ability in the past - absence of necessity - obligation - request - polite request - (im)probability - prohibition

1. This **must** be Jack's house. ......*probability (I think)*........................
2. It **can't** be 7 o'clock already! ....
3. **Shall** I open the door for you? ....

9. Functions of Modal Verbs

4. You **should** buy a new car. ....
5. You **can't** leave before 12 o'clock. ....
6. You**'d better** wash that immediately. ....
7. You **may** come in now. ....
8. **Could** I ask you a question? ....
9. He **ought to** be more careful. ....
10. There **might** be some apple pie left. ....
11. We**'ve got to** run to catch the bus. ....
12. **Would you like** me to give you a lift? ....
13. **Can** you pass me the salt, please? ....
14. I **must** go to the dentist's. ....
15. You **can** leave your coat here. ....
16. You **mustn't** tell anyone what happened. ....
17. **I'll** answer the phone for you. ....
18. He **could** play the piano when he was young. ....
19. She **needn't** wait for us. ....
20. **Do I have** to come with you? ....
21. Neil **may** not remember my phone number. ....
22. I **didn't need to** go to the bank yesterday. ....
23. You **must** listen to your parents! ....
24. He **may** know something about it. ....

136) <u>Rewrite the sentences using the words given in bold type.</u>

1. It isn't necessary to buy a ticket.
   NEED *...You don't need to buy a ticket...*
2. I advise him to be more careful.
   OUGHT ....
3. I think that's John's car.
   MUST ....
4. I don't think he is her brother.
   CAN'T ....
5. He couldn't swim when he was five.
   ABLE ....
6. It's possible that he will win the race.
   MIGHT ....
7. You are not allowed to play in their garden.
   MUSTN'T.. ....
8. It wasn't necessary for them to repair the car.
   NEED ....
9. Shall I pour you another drink?
   WOULD ....

10. It's not possible for you to eat so much.
    CAN'T ....
11. Do you want me to open the window?
    SHALL ....
12. It's just possible she's still at work.
    COULD ....
13. Do you want me to help you with that?
    WOULD ....
14. I don't think she is the woman who spoke to me.
    CAN'T ....
15. We don't have to go shopping with Mum.
    NEEDN'T ....
16. Is it really possible that she's 50 years old?
    CAN ....
17. It would be a good idea to tell him the truth.
    BETTER ....
18. I advise you to study harder.
    SHOULD ....

9. Functions of Modal Verbs

137 Put a tick according to register.

	friendly	more polite	formal	more formal
1. Can you help me please?	✓			
2. Could you help me please?				
3. May I use your phone?				
4. Might I use your phone?				
5. Can I use your phone?				
6. You can sit with us.				
7. You may sit with us.				
8. You can't stay up late.				
9. You may not sit with us.				
10. Would you like me to help you?				
11. Shall I help you?				
12. Can I have some more tea?				
13. Could I have some more tea?				

138 Fill in the correct modal verb and the speech situations as in the example:

1. You ... *shouldn't* ... eat so much. (... *advice* ....)

2. I'm an astronaut; I .... wear a uniform. (................)

3. Take your umbrella; it .... rain. (................)

4. I .... get up early on Sundays. (................)

5. You .... play football in the street. (................)

6. Children .... pay to get in. (................)

9. Functions of Modal Verbs

7. .... I come in? (..................)

8. .... I help you with the painting? (..................)

9. What .... you like to drink, sir? (..................)

10. .... you stop making that noise? (..................)

11. You .... sit with us if you like. (..................)

12. You .... buy a new suit. (..................)

Oral Activity 17

The teacher divides the class into two teams, then he/she says a modal verb and its function. The teams in turn make sentences using the verbs given. Each correct sentence gets 1 point.

Teacher: mustn't - prohibition	Teacher: can't - prohibition
Team A S1: You mustn't park your car here.	Team A S2: I can't swim.
Teacher: can - ability	Teacher: No! You can't enter that room.
Team B S1: I can ride a bicycle.	Team A doesn't get a point.

Writing Activity 12

Write the instructions the scout leader gives to the boy-scouts who are going camping.

Do	**Don't**
put name tags on their clothes	bring tobacco
bring their own sleeping bags	leave the camp alone
bring some pocket money	leave valuables in tents
bring first aid kit	
If they want	**If they don't want**
bring cassette player/walkman	join in all activities
bring own sports equipment	attend daily exercise class
invite family to visit	

Well boys, before we go off to camp, there are a few things I have to tell you. First of all, you must put name tags on your clothes and ...

10. Questions – Question Words – Question Tags

We use **do / does** to form questions in Present Simple and **did** to form questions in Past Simple.	**Does he** play the violin? **Did he** come to work yesterday?
To form questions with auxiliary verbs (**can**, **be**, **will**, **shall**, **must** etc) we put the auxiliary verb **before** the subject.	**Is he** rich? **Has he** got a car? **Will he** marry her? **Can you** fly a helicopter?
Wh-questions begin with a question word and follow the above rules (question words: **who**, **where**, **when**, **what**, **why**, **how**, **which** etc.)	**Who** is she? **What** did she do last night? **Why** did you come late?
Whose is used to express possession. **Which** is used when there is a limited choice.	**Whose** shoes are these? They're Tom's. **Which** car is yours? The red one.
The preposition goes at the end of the question.	Who does it belong **to**? Who did you go out **with**?

139 Write questions about the statements using the words in brackets.

1. He hates pizza. (pasta) — ..Does he hate pasta too?....
2. She goes to parties. (How often)
3. They went to London. (When)
4. She is crying. (Why)
5. Peter can swim. (dive)
6. John hasn't arrived yet. (Who)
7. She'll do the cleaning. (washing-up)

10. Questions - Question Words - Question Tags

8. Paula works in an office. (Where) ....

We normally use the following question words when asking about:

people	jobs / things / animals / actions	place	time	quantity	manner	reason
Who Whose Which (one of)	What Which (one of)	Where	When How long What time How often	How much How many	How	Why

140 Fill in: who, whose, what, which, where, when, how long, how often, what time, why, how much or how many

1. *Whose* is this coat? Mine.
2. .... is Robert? Julie's brother.
3. .... does the party start? At 8.30.
4. .... does this cost? £25.
5. .... is your book? The red one.
6. .... was he late? Because he overslept.
7. .... did he give you? A birthday card.
8. .... does he visit his parents? Every Monday.
9. .... eggs do you need? Ten.
10. .... is Sue's house? Next to the bank.
11. .... will you be in Paris? About a week.

Subject questions

If **who**, **which** or **what** are the subject of the question, we put the verb in the affirmative.

subject		object
Chris	helped	Mary.

Who helped Mary? (not: Who did help Mary?)

subject		object
Mary	helped	George.

Who did Mary help?

141 Write questions to which the bold type words are the answers.

1. **Sam** met Julie. ...*Who met Julie?*...
2. Roger spoke to **Jean**.
3. **Ella** phoned Stuart.
4. Jenny will see **Rosie**.
5. Steve has left a message for **Jim**.
6. Ted loves **Mary**.
7. **Pam** will visit Tom.
8. Joanne is marrying **Richard**.
9. He is talking to **her**.
10. They come from **Italy**.
11. Jim is waiting for **Tom**.

10. Questions - Question Words - Question Tags

12. Rosa is writing to **her cousin**.   ....
13. He's worried about **the test**.   ....

142 Fill in: what, how long, when, how, how much, how old, why or where.

At the Police station

Policeman : Good morning madam. 1) ....*What*.... can I do for you?
  Mrs Lee : Oh, officer, it's my Ned. He's run away from home.
Policeman : 2) .... do you live?
  Mrs Lee : At 14, Church Road.
Policeman : 3) .... is your full name?
  Mrs Lee : Jennifer Rose Lee.
Policeman : 4) .... did you last see Ned?
  Mrs Lee : At 6 o'clock yesterday evening.
Policeman : 5) .... did he seem? Was he acting strangely?
  Mrs Lee : No, not at all. He seemed completely normal.
Policeman : 6) .... is Ned?
  Mrs Lee : He's twelve.
Policeman : 7) .... money did he have?
  Mrs Lee : None. 8) .... do you ask?
Policeman : Well, because he can't have gone very far without any money.
  Mrs Lee : 9) .... will it take you to find him?
Policeman : I can't say exactly, Mrs Lee, but I hope we'll find him very soon. Now can you tell me 10) .... Ned is like?
  Mrs Lee : Certainly. He's got long floppy ears, a short tail and ...
Policeman : 11) ....? You mean Ned isn't your son, he's your dog!

143 Complete the dialogue.

Phil : 1) ..*How was your holiday?*..
Flo : It was really great!
Phil : 2) ....?
Flo : To Cairo, in Egypt.
Phil : 3) ....?
Flo: I went for a week.
Phil : 4) ....?
Flo : With my brother, Simon.
Phil : 5) ....?
Flo : We flew from London direct to Cairo.
Phil : 6) ....?
Flo : In a big hotel, right next to the Nile.
Phil : 7) ....?
Flo : We saw the Pyramids of course.
Phil : 8) ....?
Flo : We went on a boat trip along the Nile, too. That was fantastic!
Phil : 9) ....?
Flo : We arrived home last night, but I wish we had stayed longer.

10. Questions - Question Words - Question Tags

144 Look at the picture and ask your partner two questions about each boy.

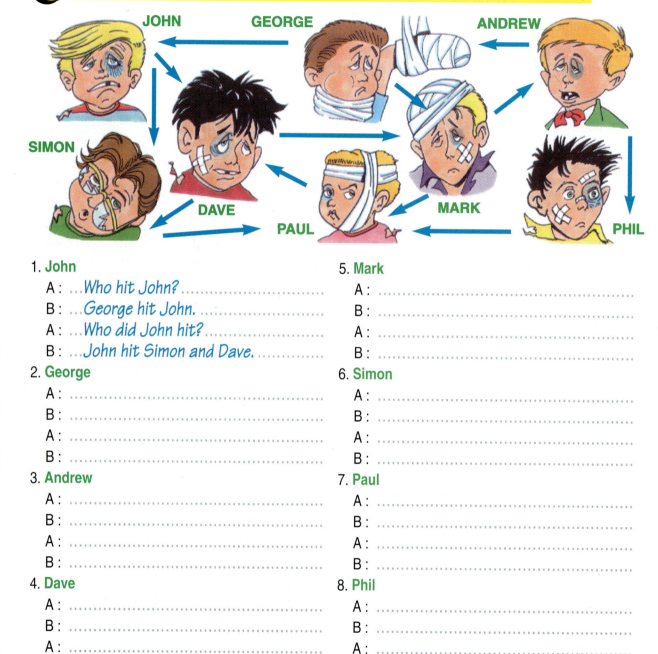

1. **John**
   A: ...Who hit John?
   B: ...George hit John.
   A: ...Who did John hit?
   B: ...John hit Simon and Dave.

2. **George**
   A:
   B:
   A:
   B:

3. **Andrew**
   A:
   B:
   A:
   B:

4. **Dave**
   A:
   B:
   A:
   B:

5. **Mark**
   A:
   B:
   A:
   B:

6. **Simon**
   A:
   B:
   A:
   B:

7. **Paul**
   A:
   B:
   A:
   B:

8. **Phil**
   A:
   B:
   A:
   B:

145 Write questions to which the bold type words are the answers.

A woman was murdered **at the Park Hotel last night**. **A maid** discovered her body. She found it in **the laundry room**. The police are looking **for the woman's husband**. **They think he did it**. He left the hotel **at 1.35 this morning**. He took all his **wife's jewellery and £1,000** from their hotel safety-deposit box. The woman's name was **Carol Webster**.

1. ...Who was murdered?
2.
3.
4.

10. Questions - Question Words - Question Tags

5. .... 8. ....
6. .... 9. ....
7. .... 10. ....

Question Tags

1. **Question tags** are short questions put at the end of a statement. We use them, not to ask for information, but for confirmation of or agreement to our statement.
   He can drive, **can't he**?

2. We form question tags with an auxiliary verb and a personal pronoun (I, you, he, it etc). A question tag has the same auxiliary verb as in the statement. If there is no auxiliary verb in the statement, we use **do**, **does** or **did** accordingly.
   She **is** sleeping, **isn't** she?
   He **came** too late, **didn't** he?

3. A **positive** statement is followed by a **negative** question tag, and a **negative** statement by a **positive** question tag.
   He **likes** apples, **doesn't** he?
   She **doesn't** like apples, **does** she?
   He **never** complains, **does** he?

4. If we **are sure** of what we are asking and we don't expect an answer, the **voice goes down** (falling intonation). If we **are not sure** and we expect an answer, the **voice goes up** (rising intonation).

   She is ugly, **isn't she**? ↘ (sure)
   She is a secretary, **isn't she**? ↗
   (not sure)

Study the following question tags.

1. "I am"	"aren't I?"	I am tall, **aren't I**?
2. "I used to"	"didn't I?"	He **used to** drive to work, **didn't he**?
3. Imperative	"will / won't you / can you / could you?"	Please **help** me, **will you / can you / could you**? Don't take all the money, **will you**?
4. "Let's"	"shall we?"	Let's make a snowman, **shall we**?
5. "Let me/him" etc	"will / won't you?"	**Let him** come with us, **will you / won't you**?
6. "I have" (= possess)	"haven't I?"	He **has** a pen, **hasn't he**?
7. "I have" (used idiomatically)	"don't / doesn't / didn't I?"	He **had** an accident last week, **didn't he**? He **has** lunch at 12.00, **doesn't he**?
8. "There is/are"	"isn't /aren't there?"	**There's** no one here, **is there**? There are a few oranges, **aren't there**?

(146) Add question tags to the following statements.

1. You're allergic to cats, *aren't you*?
2. She lives near the bank, ...?
3. Tom works at the hospital, ...?
4. Peter hasn't got a new car, ...?
5. They're journalists, ...?
6. She's in France at the moment, ...?
7. He didn't lose the keys, ...?
8. She won't help you, ...?
9. The boys weren't hurt, ...?
10. She used to eat a lot of sweets, ...?
11. Let's play football, ...?
12. They've already painted the house, ...?
13. I am tall, ...?
14. He has dinner at 6.00, ...?

10. Questions - Question Words - Question Tags

147 Add question tags to the following statements.

1. Let me help you, *will you / won't you* ?
2. Ann called Sam, ... ?
3. She won't tell us the truth, ... ?
4. Go out, ... ?
5. Sally has a pet cat, ... ?
6. They aren't going to Paris, ... ?
7. She can sing well, ... ?
8. Paul will do the shopping, ... ?
9. He never speaks rudely, ... ?
10. Let's clean the room, ... ?
11. Mary didn't use to smoke so much, ... ?
12. She has breakfast at 7.30, ... ?
13. Let me buy you this shirt, ... ?
14. John spoke to Nick, ... ?
15. Helen wears contact lenses, ... ?
16. I am thin, ... ?

148 Add questions and short answers as in the example :

1. Ben sits at the back of the class, *doesn't he* ? Yes, *he does* .
2. He's got dark brown hair, ... ? No, ... That's Bill.
3. He wears glasses, ... ? Yes, ...
4. Andrew's friend is Joe, ... ? Yes, ...
5. They talk a lot in class, ... ? Yes, ...
6. You taught them last year, ... ? Yes, unfortunately ....
7. Christine's in the same class, ... ? Yes, that's right, ...
8. She never talks, ... ? No, ...
9. Her parents are British, ... ? No, ... They're French.
10. She's the best student in the class, ... ? Yes, ...

149 Tick sure/not sure according to your teacher's intonation.

SURE	NOT SURE	
	✔	1. You can take the train, can't you? ↗
		2. He'll bring his wife, won't he?
		3. Those shoes are too big, aren't they?
		4. Your friends won't come tomorrow, will they?
		5. They were on the same plane as us, weren't they?
		6. You don't understand the exercise, do you?
		7. Prince Andrew and Sarah are divorced now, aren't they?
		8. You're not busy tonight, are you?
		9. Look, that's the President, isn't it?
		10. They live next door, don't they?
		11. Dorothy lost her purse last night, didn't she?
		12. He's got beautiful blue eyes, hasn't he?
		13. Ann can't dance, can she?
		14. William Shakespeare didn't die in 1621, did he?
		15. This coat belongs to Abi, doesn't it?
		16. Daphne got married last year, didn't she?

10. Questions - Question Words - Question Tags

Oral Activity 18

The teacher divides the class into two teams and asks them to read the text below. Then the teams in turn make statements with tag questions and give short answers about the text. Each correct question tag or short answer gets 1 point. The team with the most points is the winner.

It was Sam's birthday yesterday. He was thirteen. At 10 o'clock yesterday he caught the bus into town. He went to meet his father at the office. Then they went to buy Sam's birthday present, a guitar. Sam loves playing the guitar. He used to borrow his sister's guitar. His sister didn't like it. He is going to start having regular guitar lessons now that he has his own guitar. He hopes to be a famous guitarist for a pop group when he grows up.

Team A S1 : It was Sam's birthday yesterday, wasn't it?
Team B S1 : Yes, it was.
Team B S2 : He was fourteen, wasn't he?

Team A S2: Yes, he was.
Teacher : No, he wasn't. Team A doesn't get a point.

Oral Activity 19

The teacher divides the class into two teams and asks the students to read the text below. Then, the teams in turn ask and answer questions about the text. Each correct question and answer gets 1 point. The team with the most points is the winner.

Ann Roberts is a rich and famous singer. She lives in a big house in California. She started singing when she was 10 years old. She first sang at parties for her friends and family. Ann had to leave school at sixteen and get a job because her parents were poor. She worked in a restaurant for two years. One evening, when she was working, a friend told her about a singing competition she had seen in a newspaper she had been reading that morning. Ann entered the competition and won it! She became a star because she could sing so well.
Now she doesn't have to work in a restaurant any more and she is very happy. This year she has visited ten different countries! At the moment she is visiting Italy.

Team A S1 : Who is Ann Roberts?
Team B S1 : A rich and famous singer.

Team B S2 : Where does she live?
Team A S2 : In a big house in California. etc.

Writing Activity 13

Using the text about Ann Roberts, write an interview with her.

11. Infinitive (to + verb) – Gerund (verb + ing)

The full infinitive (inf. with to) is used:

1. to express **purpose**.
   He went **to buy** some bread.

2. after **would love** / **like** / **prefer**.
   I'**d love to see** you tonight.

3. after adjectives (**angry**, **glad**, **happy**, **sorry**, **pleased**, **annoyed**, etc).
   I'm **glad to see** you here.

4. with **too** or **enough**.
   He's **too old to drive**.
   She's clever **enough to understand** it.

5. after certain verbs (**advise**, **agree**, **appear**, **decide**, **expect**, **hope**, **manage**, **offer**, **promise**, **refuse**, **seem**, **want**, etc).
   I **hope to meet** him again.

6. after question words (**where**, **how**, **what**, **who**, **which**). **Why** is not used with to - infinitive.
   I don't know **what to do**.
   BUT Nobody knew **why** he was angry.

The bare infinitive (inf. without to) is used:

1. after **modal verbs** (can, must etc).
   We **must leave** soon.

2. after **let** / **make** / **hear** / **see** + **object**.
   Let me **go** or I'll **make** you **regret** it.

The -ing form is used:

1. as a **noun**.
   Smoking is dangerous.

2. after **love**, **like**, **dislike**, **hate**, **enjoy**.
   I **love going** to discos.

3. after **start**, **begin**, **stop**, **finish**.
   He **started doing** his homework at 5:00.

4. after **go** for physical activities.
   She **went skiing** last Sunday.

5. after certain verbs (**avoid**, **admit**, **confess to**, **deny**, **look forward to**, **mind**, **object to**, **prefer**, **regret**, **risk**, **spend**, **suggest**, etc).
   I **don't mind helping** you with the dishes.

6. after the expressions: **I'm busy**, **it's no use**, **it's (no) good**, **it's worth**, **what's the use of**, **be used to**, **there's no point (in)**.
   It's worth seeing that film.

7. after **prepositions**.
   He left **without taking** his coat.

8. after **hear**, **see**, **feel** to emphasize an action in progress.
   I saw her **crossing** the street.

11. Infinitive (to + verb) - Gerund (verb + ing)

NOTE

1) Some verbs can take a full infinitive or the -ing form with no difference in meaning. These verbs are: **begin, hate, like, love, prefer, start** etc.   e.g. He likes **to watch / watching** the birds.

2) If the subject of the verb is the same as the subject of the infinitive, then the subject of the infinitive is omitted. If, however, the subject of the verb is different from the subject of the infinitive, then an object pronoun (me, you, him etc) is placed before the infinitive.
Compare: I want to be back at 10 o'clock.   I want **him** to be back at 10 o'clock.

150 Write what each word is followed by: F.I. (full infinitive), B.I. (bare infinitive) or -ing.

1. want   + ..F.I..
2. dislike   + ...
3. would love   + ...
4. it's worth   + ...
5. finish   + ...
6. will   + ...
7. make   + ...
8. avoid   + ...
9. see   + ...
10. promise   + ...
11. expect   + ...
12. it's no use + ...
13. hope   + ...
14. let   + ...
15. shall   + ...
16. can   + ...
17. start   + ...
18. deny   + ...
19. hate   + ...
20. must   + ...

151 Put the verbs in brackets into the correct form.

Yesterday I went with my sister 1) ..to buy.. (buy) something for her birthday. She didn't really know what 2) .... (get) but she seemed 3) .... (like) the idea of a pet, so we went to the nearest pet shop. She started 4) .... (look) around at all the animals. The man in the shop let her 5) .... (pick up) the rabbits and stroke the hamsters, but when she saw some puppies 6) .... (play) in a box, she said that she would like 7) .... (have) one of them.
I didn't know if we had enough money 8) .... (buy) one and I hoped my mother wouldn't object to 9) .... (have) a dog in the house, but my sister promised 10) .... (look after) it properly and we did have enough money, so we bought a little black dog. The man gave us a special brush for 11) .... (brush) him and some special food. Tomorrow we're going to take Splash to the beach.

152 Put the verbs in brackets into the correct form.

Dear Julie,
I am writing 1) ..to thank.... (thank) you for my birthday present. I was so happy 2) .... (receive) it - I had so many lovely presents, I don't know what 3) .... (do) with them all! On my birthday I went for a meal with some friends and afterwards we went 4) .... (dance) at that new club on Poplar Street. If you haven't been, it's certainly worth 5) .... (go) there.
Now that I'm old enough 6) .... (drive), I'm busy 7) .... (take) driving lessons. Dad has said he'll let me 8) .... (use) his car as long as I promise 9) .... (be) careful.
Well, I must 10) .... (go) now. I hope 11) .... (hear) from you soon.
                                        Love,
                                        Madeleine

11. Infinitive (to + verb) - Gerund (verb + ing)

153 Put the verbs in brackets in the infinitive or the -ing form.

1. I don't like ...*singing/to sing*........ in public. (sing)
2. It's no use .... her. She won't listen. (tell)
3. I'm still too upset .... about it. (talk)
4. Don't disturb him. He's busy .... (work)
5. Stop .... your nails! (bite)
6. Don't expect him .... you any money. (lend)
7. I've decided .... him. (leave)
8. Mum made me .... my medicine. (take)
9. She agreed .... him £1,000. (lend)
10. He denied .... the stolen goods. (receive)

The black shoes are *too big*. The red shoes are *too expensive*. The green shoes are *not cheap enough*.

Too + adjective/adverb (negative implication)	He's **too young** to have a car. (He's **so young** that he **can't have** a car.)
Adjective/adverb + enough (positive implication)	She's **clever enough** to do the exercise. (She **can do** the exercise.) It's **early enough** for us to catch the bus. (It's **quite early** so we **can still catch** the bus.)
Enough + noun	He's got **enough courage** to do it.

154 Answer the questions using too or enough.

1. Can he run fast? (fat)
   ...*No, he is too fat*........

2. Can she eat all the cake? (big)
   No, ...

3. Can he lift the car? (heavy)
   No, ...

4. Can he jump over the fence? (young) No, ...

5. Can he make people laugh? (funny) Yes, ...

6. Can he sleep in this bed? (small) No, ...

11. Infinitive (to + verb) - Gerund (verb + ing)

155 Put the verbs in brackets into the infinitive or -ing form.

My mother is an amazing woman. She is 87 years old and she still enjoys 1) ...*going out*... (go out) for a walk every day. She doesn't mind 2) .... (do) all her housework and she's glad 3) .... (help) her elderly neighbours when they can't 4) .... (go) to the shops. She's too old 5) .... (dig) the garden any more – she stopped 6) .... (do) that last year – but she's still healthy enough 7) .... (mow) the grass! In the summer she still goes 8) .... (swim) when it's warm and she lets her grandchildren 9) .... (bury) her in the sand. She often says, "It's no good 10) .... (be) alive if you don't enjoy yourself." I'd love 11) .... (be) like my mother when I'm her age.

Oral Activity 20

The teacher divides the class into two teams and says words or phrases which are followed by the infinitive or gerund. The teams in turn make sentences. Each correct sentence gets 1 point.

| Teacher : | refuse | Teacher : | it's no use |
| Team A S1 : | John refused to help me. | Team B S1 : | It's no use telling lies. etc. |

Oral Activity 21

The students work in groups of three for 3 minutes making up a story by using the pictures and the list of words given. Finally they report their story to the teacher.

enjoyed, suggested, began, too late, was busy, what, expect, regretted, too angry

Writing Activity 14

Look at the pictures for Oral Activity 21 then listen to your teacher read out the story twice. Finally write the story you've just heard. (80 - 100 words)

12. The Passive

Look at all the dust in here! It looks as if this room hasn't been cleaned for a month!

Well, don't blame me! I was only hired a week ago.

The passive is formed with the appropriate tense of the verb **to be + past participle**.

	Active Voice	Passive Voice
Present Simple	He **delivers** letters.	Letters **are delivered**.
Past Simple	He **delivered** the letters.	The letters **were delivered**.
Present Perfect	He **has delivered** the letters.	The letters **have been delivered**.
Future Simple	He **will deliver** the letters.	The letters **will be delivered**.
Past Perfect	He **had delivered** the letters.	The letters **had been delivered**.
Present Continuous	He **is delivering** the letters.	The letters **are being delivered**.
Past Continuous	He **was delivering** the letters.	The letters **were being delivered**.
Infinitive	He has **to deliver** the letters.	The letters have **to be delivered**.
Modals (Modal + be + past part.)	He **may deliver** the letters.	The letters **may be delivered**.
	He **must deliver** the letters.	The letters **must be delivered**.

The Passive is used :

1. when the **agent** (= the person who does the action) is **unknown**, **unimportant** or **obvious** from the context.
   Jane **was shot**. (We don't know who shot her.)
   This church **was built** in 1815. (unimportant agent)
   He **has been arrested**. (obviously by the police)

2. to make more **polite** or **formal** statements.
   The car **hasn't been cleaned**. (more polite)
   (You haven't cleaned the car. – less polite)

3. when the **action is more important** than the agent, as in processes, instructions, events, reports, headlines, news items, and advertisements.
   30 people **were killed** in the earthquake.

4. to put **emphasis on the agent**.
   The new library will be opened **by the Queen**.

12. The Passive

156 Put the verbs in brackets into Present Simple Passive.

There is a chimpanzee which 1) *is called* (call) "Bubbles". It 2) .... (own) by Michael Johnson. It 3) .... (keep) in his home. It 4) .... (feed) every day by Michael Johnson himself. It 5) .... (always/dress) in funny clothes. It 6) .... (say) that "Bubbles" is Michael Johnson's only friend.

157 Look at the Hotel Information table and write sentences as in the example:

HOTEL INFORMATION	
BREAKFAST - In Pierrot's Restaurant 7-9.30 am	**ROOMS -** Maid Service daily
DINNER - In Main Restaurant 8-10 pm	**HOT WATER -** 24 hours a day
NEWSPAPERS - TELEPHONE CALLS At the Reception Desk	**HOTEL CINEMA -** Film every night at 10 pm

1. Breakfast / serve - where and when?
   Breakfast is served in Pierrot's Restaurant between 7 and 9.30 am.
2. Dinner / serve - where and when?
   ....
3. Newspapers / sell - where?
   ....
4. Telephone calls / can make - where?
   ....
5. Rooms / clean - who by and how often?
   ....
6. Hot water / supply - when?
   ....
7. Films / show - where and when?
   ....

158 Put the verbs in brackets into Past Simple Passive.

Two men 1) *were seen* (see) breaking into a house in my street last night. The police 2) .... (call) and they arrived very quickly. One man 3) .... (catch) immediately. The other escaped, but he 4) .... (find) very soon. Both men 5) .... (take) to the police station where they 6) .... (question) separately by a police officer. The two men 7) .... (charge) with burglary.

12. The Passive

159 Rewrite the newspaper headlines as complete sentences.

1. FOOTBALLER OFFERED MILLION FOR TRANSFER
2. NO CHILDREN ADMITTED INTO SPORTS CLUB
3. CHILDREN BEING BRAINWASHED BY TV
4. PLANET BEING DESTROYED BY POLLUTION
5. BOMB DISCOVERED IN OLD LADY'S GARDEN
6. NO CAMERAS ALLOWED IN MUSEUM
7. ANIMALS BEING USED TO TEST BEAUTY PRODUCTS
8. PICASSO PAINTINGS EXHIBITED NATIONAL GALLERY NEXT MONDAY
9. MICHAEL JACKSON ASKED TO SPONSOR CHARITY EVENT YESTERDAY

1. *The footballer has been offered a million pounds for the transfer.*
2.
3.
4.
5.
6.
7.
8.
9.

160 Fill in the correct passive form.

Mr Pryce was having his house done up. Write what he saw when he went to inspect the work.

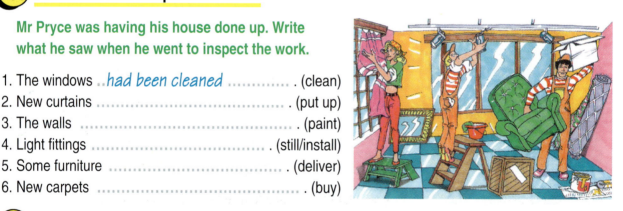

1. The windows *had been cleaned* . (clean)
2. New curtains .... (put up)
3. The walls .... (paint)
4. Light fittings .... (still/install)
5. Some furniture .... (deliver)
6. New carpets .... (buy)

161 Fill in the Passive in the appropriate tense, then justify its use.

action more important than the agent, unknown agent, unimportant agent, emphasis on the agent, polite statement, obvious agent

1. *emphasis on the agent*   2. ....   3. ....

(TV/invent/Baird)   (Pyramids/build/Egyptians)   (milk/produce/cows)

TV was invented by Baird.

12. The Passive

Changing from Active into Passive

The object of the active verb becomes the subject in the new sentence.
The active verb changes into a passive form and the subject

	Subject	Verb	Object	(agent)
Active	Picasso	painted	that picture.	
Passive	That picture	was painted		by Picasso.

of the active verb becomes the agent. The agent is introduced with **by** or it is omitted.

After modal verbs (**will, can, must, have to, should, may, ought to**) we use **be + past participle**.
You **can** use the machine for cutting bread. ➡ The machine **can be used** for cutting bread.

With verbs taking two objects it is more usual to begin the passive sentence with the person.
I sent **her** some roses. **She** was sent some roses. (more usual) or **Some roses** were sent to her. (less usual)

We put the agent (= the person who does the action) into the passive sentence only if it adds information. When the agent is unknown, unimportant or obvious it is omitted. Agents such as **people** (in general), **they**, **somebody** etc. are omitted.
Bell invented the telephone.
The telephone was invented **by Bell**. (The agent is not omitted because it adds information.)
Somebody murdered him. He was murdered (~~by somebody~~). (Unknown agent is omitted.)
The police arrested him. He was arrested (~~by the police~~). (Obvious agent is omitted.)

162) Turn from Active into Passive.

1. The gardener has planted some trees. *Some trees have been planted by the gardener.*
2. Doctor Brown will give you some advice. ....
3. A famous designer will redecorate the hotel. ....
4. Steven Spielberg directed "E.T." ....

163) Turn from Active into Passive. Omit the agent where it can be omitted.

1. Someone has broken the crystal vase. *The crystal vase has been broken. (omitted)*
2. His parents have brought him up to be polite. ....
3. Fleming discovered penicillin. ....
4. They will advertise the product on television. ....
5. Someone is remaking that film. ....

164) Using the Passive, ask questions to which the bold type words are answers.

1. **Columbus** discovered America.   *Who was America discovered by* ?
2. We keep money **in a safe**.   .... ?
3. **A bee** stung him.   .... ?
4. They speak **Italian** in Italy.   .... ?
5. They have taken **his aunt** to hospital. .... ?
6. **The boys** damaged the television.   .... ?

7. **Da Vinci** painted the Mona Lisa. ....?
8. He invited **30 people** to his party. ....?
9. They grow bananas **in Africa**. ....?

165 Turn from Active into Passive.

1. You must leave the bathroom tidy. *The bathroom must be left tidy.*
2. You should water this plant daily. ....
3. Our neighbour ought to paint the garage. ....
4. I have to return these books to the library. ....

166 Turn from Active into Passive as in the example:

1. He gave me a present.
   I was given a present. (more usual)
   A present was given to me. (less usual)
2. The waiter will bring us the bill.
   ....
3. The Queen presented him with a medal.
   ....

4. Her mother bought Mary some sweets.
   ....
5. Bob has sold Ted a second-hand car.
   ....
6. Larry is going to send a letter to Tom.
   ....

167 Turn from Active into Passive.

1. Someone is helping her with the housework. *She is being helped with the housework.*
2. A pickpocket robbed me. ....
3. You must extinguish your cigarettes. ....
4. The mail-order company sent Mrs Green a parcel. ....
5. You must dry-clean this shirt. ....
6. Someone will pay you within the next few days. ....
7. You can improve your health with more exercise. ....
8. A dog is chasing the child. ....

168 Turn from Active into Passive.

1. My friend sent me an invitation. *I was sent an invitation.*
2. The cleaner is going to mop the kitchen floor. ....
3. The farmer is building a new barn. ....
4. The secretary has given Mrs Jones some letters. ....
5. The traffic warden had already given him a ticket for illegal parking. ....
6. People must obey the law. ....
7. Someone had broken our door down. ....
8. They chose him as the best actor of the year. ....

12. The Passive

169 **A reporter is talking to Lucy Fame. Complete the interview.**

Rep: It's wonderful to interview such a famous person as you.
Lucy: Yes, you are very lucky!
Rep: I know that you 1) ......*have been interviewed*......... (interview) many times before.
Lucy: Yes, I have.
Rep: Also, I know that three books 2) .... (write) about you.
Lucy: Yes, they have – and another one 3) .... (write) at the moment.
Rep: A film 4) .... (make) about your life two years ago, wasn't it?
Lucy: Yes, it was a brilliant film! The leading role 5) .... (play) by a beautiful young actress.
Rep: 6) .... any more films .... (make) in the future?
Lucy: Oh yes, of course!
Rep: Where do you buy your clothes from, Lucy?
Lucy: I don't buy them! They 7) .... (design) especially for me.
Rep: And what about your beautiful house?
Lucy: That 8) .... (build) five years ago by an Italian architect.
Rep: You must make a lot of money.
Lucy: I make lots of money and everybody loves me. Flowers 9) .... (send) to my house every day.
Rep: Not by me, that's certain!

170 **Rewrite the following passage in the Passive.**

Some people saw a UFO in the sky above London last night. They reported it to the police. The army sent a helicopter to look at it more closely. The UFO shot the helicopter down and killed both men in it. People have given photographs of the UFO to the police. Experts are looking at them now.

171 **Rewrite the following passage in the Passive.**

Somebody has stolen a bus from outside the school. Some children saw the thief. The police are searching for the bus now. They will use the children's descriptions to catch the thief.

12. The Passive

172 Rewrite the following passage in the Passive.

Someone broke into a local jewellery shop yesterday. The owner had just locked up the shop when a robber with a gun threatened him. The robber told him to unlock the shop and give him all the diamonds in the safe. Then the robber tied him up. The police have organised a search for the robber. They hope they will find him in a few days. Doctors are treating the owner of the shop for shock.

173 Rewrite the following passage in the Passive.

My uncle painted this picture. Someone has offered him a lot of money for it. He will deliver the painting tomorrow. When they give him the money he will tell them the truth. He painted it one night while he was sleepwalking!

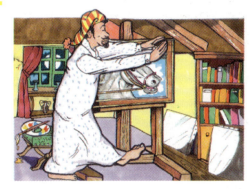

174 Rewrite the following passage in the Passive.

Our school is organising a contest. The teachers will choose the best project about the environment. The students must include pictures and drawings in their projects. The students will also have to do all the writing themselves. The school will give the winner a set of encyclopaedias.

Writing Activity 15

Write a news report in the Passive using the notes below.

A small Japanese village - hit - earthquake - last night. It - think - there are few survivors. The time of the disaster - give - as 7.00 p.m. The village - destroy - the force of the earthquake. Soldiers - send - to the village - the Government to help in the search for survivors. Efforts - still - make to clear the village. Further help - give - the Government soon. Since the survivors are homeless they - take - to the next village. Any further news - give - to you as it arrives.

13. Conditionals

Type 1	If - clause	Main clause (result)	Use
real present	If + Present S. unless (= if not)	Future Imperative can/must/may + bare infinitive Present Simple	real or very probable situation in the present or future

If he **comes** late, we**'ll miss** the bus.
If you **can't afford** it, **don't buy** it.   or   Unless you **can** afford it, **don't buy** it.
If you **see** her, **can you give** her a message?
If water **gets** very cold, it **turns** into ice.

Type 2	If - clause	Main clause (result)	Use
unreal present	if + Past S.	would/could/might + bare infinitive	improbable situation in the present or future; also used to give advice

If I **were** you, I **would see** a doctor. (advice)
If I **had** money, I **could buy** a new car. (But I don't have enough money to buy one.) (improbable situation)

Type 3	If - clause	Main clause (result)	Use
unreal past	if + Past Perfect	would/could/might + have + past participle	unreal or improbable situation in the past; also used to express regrets and criticism

If you **hadn't been** rude, he **wouldn't have fired** you. (But you were very rude and he fired you.) (criticism)

13. Conditionals

Study the following notes :

1. We put a comma after the if-clause when it comes first.
   If we go by plane, it will be more expensive.
   It will be more expensive if we go by plane.

2. **Unless** means **if not**.
   We'll go for a picnic **unless** it rains.
   We'll go for a picnic **if** it does**n't** rain.

3. After if, we can use **were** instead of **was** in all persons.
   If I **were** you, I wouldn't spend so much money.

4. We do not usually use **will**, **would** or **should** in an if-clause.
   If **we take** a taxi, we won't be late.
   NOT If we will take a taxi, we won't be late.
   However, we use **should** after **if** when we are less sure about a possibility.
   If I see him, I'll give it to him. (Perhaps I will see him.)
   If I **should** see him, I'll give it to him. (Perhaps I'll see him but I'm less sure.)

175 Match the following parts of the sentences.

1. If I go on a diet,
2. If it's sunny tomorrow,
3. If John doesn't hurry,
4. If it snows,
5. If there are no buses,
6. If you are a good girl,

A. we'll make a snowman.
B. I'll buy you some chocolate.
C. she'll have to take a taxi.
D. I'll lose weight.
E. he'll be late.
F. we'll go for a picnic.

1. ...D............
2. ....
3. ....
4. ....
5. ....
6. ....

176 Fill in: unless or if.

1. ..If... you make so much noise, I won't be able to sleep.
2. I'll tell you .... there are any messages for you.
3. I won't finish the work .... you help me.
4. .... you're hungry, I'll make you a sandwich.
5. We'll miss the bus .... we hurry.
6. They won't get married .... he gets a job.
7. You won't understand .... you listen carefully.

177 Write real present conditionals (1st type).

1. (eat/put on weight)
   ..If he eats so much, he...
   ..will put on weight.........

2. (not/work hard/lose job)
   ....
   ....

3. (rain/stay at home)
   ....
   ....

13. Conditionals

178 Put the verbs in brackets into the correct tense. Add a comma where necessary.

1. If the dog ..*keeps*.. (keep) barking **,** the neighbours will complain.
2. The boss .... (be) angry if you arrive late for work again.
3. If you .... (eat) too much you'll be sick!
4. If the weather is bad on Saturday we .... (stay) at home.
5. You should see a doctor if you .... (not/feel) well.
6. If you study hard you .... (pass) your exam.

179 What would you do in each situation? Write unreal present conditionals.

call an ambulance, complain to the manager, run away, try to catch it,
walk to the nearest garage to get some, ring the police

1. You find a fly in your soup.
2. You see a burglar breaking into your house.
3. You see a mouse in your kitchen.

If I found a fly in my soup, I would complain to the manager.

4. Your car runs out of petrol.
5. You see an accident.
6. You see a ghost in your room.

180 Put the verbs in brackets into the correct tense.

Sarah is a bored teenager. If she 1) ..*joined*.. (join) a club, she 2) .... (make) more friends. She 3) .... (enjoy) herself if she 4) .... (go) out more. Her schoolwork is suffering too. If she 5) .... (study) more, she 6) .... (have) better marks and she 7) .... (enter) university. Unfortunately, she is becoming overweight. She 8) .... (feel) fitter if she 9) .... (start) swimming, and she 10) .... (get) thinner if she 11) .... (stop) eating so much chocolate.

13. Conditionals

181 Advise Jenny what to do in each situation.

1. J: I can't see a thing.
   Y: ...If I were you, I'd clean my glasses!...

2. J: I'm tired.
   Y: ....

3. J: I'm hungry.
   Y: ....

4. J: My skirt is too tight.
   Y: ....

5. J: My hair's a mess.
   Y: ....

6. J: I've got a toothache.
   Y: ....

182 Put the verbs in brackets into the correct tense.

If John 1) ..hadn't overslept... (not/oversleep), he 2) .... (not/be) late for work. If he 3) .... (not/be) late for work, his boss 4) .... (not/fire) him. If John 5) .... (not/lose) his job, he 6) .... (not/need) money and he 7) .... (not/rob) the bank. If he 8) .... (not/rob) the bank, the police 9) .... (not/arrest) him.

183 Write unreal past conditionals (3rd type) as in the example:

1. (climb ladder/break his leg)
   ..If he hadn't climbed the ladder, he wouldn't have broken his leg.

2. (drive carefully/avoid accident)
   ....

3. (John run faster/win the race)
   ....

13. Conditionals

184 Match the parts of the sentences.

1. If I hadn't missed the bus,
2. If she hadn't felt ill this morning,
3. If the food hadn't been awful,
4. If he had passed his exams,
5. If the salary had been good,
6. If it hadn't been my birthday,

A. he would have gone to university.
B. Chris wouldn't have given me flowers.
C. she would have gone to school.
D. I would have accepted the job.
E. I wouldn't have been late for work.
F. we would have eaten it.

1. ...E...
2. ....
3. ....
4. ....
5. ....
6. ....

185 Write real present, unreal present or unreal past conditionals. Then state the types of conditionals.

1. (smoke so much/get ill)
..If he smokes so much,..
...he'll get ill...........
...(1st type, real present).

2. (have money/buy burger)

3. (put on coat/catch cold)

4. (fall over/break plates)

5. (play with knife/cut finger)

6. (leave cupboard open/hit head)

7. (headache/take aspirin)

8. (leave fish table/cat eat it)

9. (eat so much/be fat)

13. Conditionals

186 Use Thomas's thoughts to write conditionals as in the example, then state the types of conditionals (real present, unreal present, unreal past).

Thomas is on a desert island and he is thinking.

1. I'll make a hut. I don't want to sleep under the trees.
2. I don't have a bottle. I can't send a message.
3. I didn't save the radio transmitter. I didn't call for help.
4. There are too many sharks and I can't escape.
5. I have no company. I feel lonely.
6. I'll make an axe. Then I may be able to make a raft.
7. I lost my knife in the water. I didn't cut any branches down.
8. Please let someone find me, or I'll die on this island.

1. ....If I make a hut, I won't have to sleep under the trees. (real present)...........
2. ....
3. ....
4. ....
5. ....
6. ....
7. ....
8. ....

187 Put the verbs in brackets into the correct tense.

1. If she ...*hadn't broken*.... (not / break) the window, she wouldn't have had to pay for a new one.
2. If it .... (not/be) cold, they wouldn't have lit the fire.
3. If she studied more, she .... (be) a better student.
4. They .... (not/see) the Queen if they hadn't visited London on that day.
5. If you should win that competition, you .... (be) rich.
6. If I lived in France, I .... (speak) French well.
7. If they .... (lock) the doors, the burglars wouldn't have got in.
8. We .... (have) a party if Alan passes his driving test.
9. I .... (give) John your message if I should see him today.
10. They .... (not/have) any money if their cousin hadn't lent them some.
11. Those plants .... (not/grow) if you don't water them.
12. I would buy that bag if it .... (be) cheaper.
13. If she .... (open) the letter, she would have been surprised.

101

13. Conditionals

Oral Activity 22 (Chain Story)

The students in two teams look at the picture. Then students in turn make conditionals Type 1 about the person in the picture who is pouring orange juice, as in the example:

Teacher: If he goes home late, he'll go to bed late.
Team A S1: If he goes to bed late, he won't wake up early.
Team B S1: If he doesn't wake up early, he will miss the bus.

Oral Activity 23

The students in two teams read the text and in turn make conditionals Type 3.

There was a family who was very poor so they lived in a little house. One day the children were hungry so the mother went to the market. On the way she crossed a bridge and saw something in the river. She leant over the bridge and her purse fell into the water. It sank to the bottom of the river so she couldn't reach it. A fish swam by and swallowed it. She had no money so she went home. There was no food in the house so the father went fishing. He caught a big fish so he had something for his wife to cook. She cut the fish open and found her purse inside with all the money still in it.

Team A S1 : If they hadn't been poor, they wouldn't have lived in a little house.
Team B S1 : If the children hadn't been hungry, the mother wouldn't have gone to the market.

Oral Activity 24

The teacher divides the class into two teams and asks the students to look at the picture. Then the teams in turn, using conditionals Type 2, suggest as many things as possible that would help John be healthier.

Teacher: If John went to bed earlier, he wouldn't be tired.
Team A S1: If he didn't smoke so much, he wouldn't cough.
Team B S1: If he didn't eat so many sweets, he wouldn't be so fat, etc.

Writing Activity 16

Write a letter of advice to a friend of yours who isn't very healthy. (60 - 80 words)

Dear Tom,
   You don't feel well because you eat too much. If you ate less, you would feel better ...

Revision Exercises III

188 Choose the correct item.

1. I look forward ....B.......... you soon.
   A) to see   B) to seeing   C) see

2. Bob said he .... come to the party but he isn't sure yet.
   A) should   B) might   C) needn't

3. .... umbrella is this? It's Tina's.
   A) Whose   B) Which   C) Who's

4. You .... obey your parents.
   A) must   B) have to   C) need

5. Andrew .... the kitchen since 7 o'clock.
   A) painted   B) has painted   C) has been painting

6. He suggested .... for a walk.
   A) to go   B) go   C) going

7. Are you going to Rome this year? No, I .... there twice already.
   A) went   B) have gone   C) have been

8. She .... be only 30, she looks much older.
   A) mustn't   B) can't   C) needn't

9. When I arrived at the party everyone ....
   A) danced   B) is dancing   C) was dancing

10. I'd love .... the evening with you.
    A) spend   B) spending   C) to spend

189 Find the mistake and correct it.

1. Tell the children to sit ~~quiet~~ and wait for me.   *quietly*
2. There's no point to talk to him.
3. She'll come when she will be ready.
4. She made me to stay at home.
5. Their car is more big than ours.
6. That was the worse cake I've ever eaten.
7. The bank robbers arrested yesterday.
8. This is the most cheap shirt I could find.
9. Shall we go to ski tomorrow?
10. Whose at the door?

190 Add questions and short answers as in the example:

1. Ann lives in London, ...*doesn't she*...? Yes, ...*she does*.....
2. Her daughter has moved to Swansea, ...? No, ... She's in London.
3. She isn't married, ...? Yes, ...
4. She hasn't got any children, ...? Yes, ...
5. You visited them last summer, ...? Yes, ...
6. You didn't meet Tony, ...? No, ... He was in Holland.
7. He'll be here in July, ...? No, ... He'll still be in Holland.
8. He has been there a long time, ...? Yes, ...
9. He isn't thinking of staying there, ...? Yes, ... He likes Holland a lot.
10. Ann will never agree to that, ...? No, ...

Revision Exercises III

191 Answer the questions using "too" or "enough".

1. Can he have a shower? (cold) No, ..*it's too cold.*..
2. Can he jump? (frightened) No, ...
3. Can he go to work? (well) No, ...

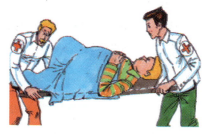  

4. Can they carry him? (strong) Yes, ...
5. Can he lift it? (strong) No, ...
6. Can Bob win? (slow) No, ...

192 Turn from Active into Passive.

1. They are giving her a promotion.   ....*She is being given a promotion.*....
2. A famous architect designed these buildings.
3. Van Gogh painted that picture.
4. Three people must sign this form.
5. The Queen will open the exhibition.
6. Lightning has struck the tree.
7. You must complete this work today.
8. Fire destroyed the forest.
9. You can improve your English with more study.

193 Turn the following passage into the Passive.

Someone found a skeleton in a cave in the mountains yesterday. They have sent it to a laboratory. Scientists were examining it all through the night. They have discovered that it is the skeleton of a dinosaur from thousands of years ago. They are still carrying out tests. They are going to send it to a museum when they have completed the tests.

Revision Exercises III

194 **Fill in : both (of), neither (of), none (of) or all (of).**

Deborah and Sally are friends. They 1) ..*both*... like skiing and mountain-climbing, but 2) .... them likes water sports, so they often go on winter holidays together. Last winter they went to Switzerland with 3) .... their friends who like skiing, and they 4) .... had a wonderful time. Unfortunately 5) .... their friends had enough money to stay more than a week, but 6) .... Deborah and Sally are planning to go again this year. 7) .... them would miss it for the world.

195 **Fill in: some, any, no or their derivatives.**

In the village where I live there is a story that 1) ....*someone*.... hid a great treasure many years ago 2) .... in the churchyard. 3) .... has ever discovered it, although many people have tried. The story also says that if 4) .... discovers the treasure, he will have 5) .... but bad luck for the rest of his life. At the end of the last century, a man from the village spent the night in the churchyard looking for the treasure. In the morning, his friends couldn't find him 6) .... Finally, after many days, he returned to the village but 7) .... could understand 8) .... he said. I am not sure if there's 9) .... truth in the story, and I don't really want to find out.

196 **Put the verbs in brackets into the correct tense.**

Last Friday, my best friend Emma 1) ....*had*.... (have) a party. She 2) .... (just/finish) school and she 3) .... (decide) to celebrate the occasion with a big party. She 4) .... (invite) all her friends and she 5) .... (buy) lots of food and drink. When the evening of the party 6) .... (arrive), she 7) .... (have) a bath and while she 8) .... (get) dressed the doorbell 9) .... (ring). She 10) .... (run) to answer it when she 11) .... (fall) over the bag of food she 12) .... (leave) in the hall and 13) .... (hurt) her leg badly. When she 14) .... (manage) to open the door, her friend Donna 15) .... (stand) there. She 16) .... (take) a look at her leg and 17) .... (say), "I 18) .... (take) you to hospital. I 19) .... (think) you 20) .... (break) your leg." When Emma 21) .... (leave) the hospital she 22) .... (walk) on crutches. She 23) .... (never/imagine) she would have such a nasty experience on a day like that.

Revision Exercises III

197 Put the verbs in brackets into the correct form.

Last year I decided 1) ..*to explore*.. (explore) the old house near our village. My little brother refused 2) .... (come) because he was frightened but my friend Geoff said he didn't mind 3) .... (go) with me. We arrived at the house late one evening and began 4) .... (climb) the old dark stairs. When we reached the top it was so dark that I couldn't see anything. To my horror Geoff seemed to have disappeared. Suddenly I heard something 5) .... (make) a strange noise which made my hair 6) .... (stand) on end. At first I thought it was Geoff who was pretending 7) .... (be) a ghost. Then Geoff appeared behind me. We were scared. We didn't know what 8) .... (do). We thought we'd better 9) .... (leave) the house quickly. When I told my parents what had happened they made me 10) .... (promise) not 11) .... (go) there again.

198 Ask questions to which the bold type words are the answers.

Fred Jones is an old man. He was born on **March 17th 1923** in **Liverpool**. He married **Julie Tosh** in 1951. She died **last year**. He felt very **lonely** when Julie died. Now he lives in **an old people's home**. Today he is celebrating his birthday **with a small party**. **The staff** have helped him organise it. **All the old people in the home** have been invited to the party and **his grandchildren** are coming this afternoon. Fred will blow out the candles on his cake **at 5 o'clock**. Unfortunately he won't eat any of the cake **because he doesn't like cake at all**.

1. ...*When was Fred Jones born?*...
2. ....
3. ....
4. ....
5. ....
6. ....
7. ....
8. ....
9. ....
10. ....
11. ....
12. ....

199 Finish the following sentences.

1. If I had enough money, ...*I'd buy a new pair of shoes.*...
2. I wouldn't say that to her ....
3. If it doesn't rain soon, ...
4. We'll stay at home ....
5. If you didn't go to the gym so often, ...
6. Unless you invite her to the party, ...
7. She wouldn't have forgotten the appointment ....
8. We would have reached the airport on time ....
9. If you drive so carelessly, ...
10. If I had got to the station earlier, ...

14. Relatives

Relative Pronouns (who, whose, whom, which, that) introduce relative clauses.

used for	subject of the verb of the relative clause (can't be omitted)	object of the verb of the relative clause (can be omitted)	possession (can't be omitted)
people	who/that	who/whom/that	whose
	She's the teacher **who/that** came to our school last week.	This is the man **(whom/that)** we hired last Monday.	That's the boy **whose** brother won the prize.
used for things/ animals	which/that	which/that	whose/of which
	This is the house **which/that** belongs to my friend.	Here's the bag **(which/that)** you left on my desk.	That's the bag **whose** handle is broken.

1. **That** replaces **who** or **which** but is never used after commas or prepositions. **That** usually follows superlatives and words like something, nothing, anything, all, none, many, few.
   Ann, **who** is very clever, did the puzzle in five minutes. ("**That**" is impossible here.)
   There's **something that** you don't know.
   She's the **tallest** girl **that** I've ever seen.

2. **Prepositions in Relative Clauses.** We avoid using prepositions before relative pronouns.
   That's the girl **with** whom I went to the party. (very formal)
   That's the girl (who/that) I went to the party **with**. (less formal, more usual)

3. **Who, whom, which, that** can be omitted when there is a noun or a pronoun (I, you, etc) between the relative pronoun and the verb, that is, when they are the objects of the relative clause.
   The clock (which/that) I bought yesterday does not work. (**Which/that** can be omitted.)
   Where is the ring (which/that) **George** gave you? (**Which/that** can be omitted.)
   A person **who** repairs cars is a mechanic. (**Who** can't be omitted).

14. Relatives

Relative Adverbs (when, where, why)

Time	when (= in/on which)	That was the summer (**when**) it rained every day.
Place	where (= in/on/at/to which)	That's the hotel **where** we stayed.
Reason	why (= for which)	Can you tell me the reason (**why**) he lied to me?

201 Fill in : who, whose, which or where.

My school, 1) ...*which*... is called King Edward's, has about 2,000 students. My favourite teacher, 2) .... is called Mr Brown, teaches sport. The sports centre, 3) .... I play basketball and tennis, is the largest in the area. I walk to school every day with my friend Mike, 4) .... father teaches me History.

202 Complete the sentences using relatives as in the example:

1. A painter is someone ..*who*.. *paints pictures.*..............
2. A supermarket is a place ....
3. A tiger is an animal ....

4. A builder is someone ....
5. A widow is a woman ....
6. You can't live in a house ....

203 Fill in: who's or whose.

1. My mother, ...*whose*...... name is Ana, is a housewife.
2. She's the woman .... moved next door.
3. Rita is the girl .... father won the lottery.
4. Helen is the person .... car was stolen.
5. Ann's the one .... lost a lot of weight.
6. Massimo is the man .... going to help me.
7. That's the woman .... son was killed in an accident.

14. Relatives

204 Fill in the correct relative pronoun. Then write S for subject and O for object. Finally state if the relatives can be omitted or not in the box provided.

1. Did you see the man ... *who* .... stole her bag?
2. The eggs .... you've bought are bad.
3. Please give me the keys .... are on the table.
4. Is that the man .... we saw in the park yesterday?
5. What's the name of the lady .... babysits for you?
6. Tom is playing with the dog .... lives next door.
7. Have you eaten all the cakes .... I made yesterday?
8. How old is the man .... owns this shop?
9. Have you met the man .... Jackie is going to marry?
10. Let's all look at the picture .... is on page 7.
11. Has Peter returned the money .... he borrowed from you?
12. What colour is the dress .... you're going to wear tonight?
13. The police have arrested the man .... murdered his wife.
14. The parcel .... is on the table is your birthday present.
15. We will ask the man .... delivers our milk to leave an extra bottle.
16. Is she the person .... gave you this record?
17. We spent our holiday in a small town .... is near the sea.
18. The man .... married Kate is a millionaire.
19. Where are the shoes .... I bought this morning?
20. I still write to that lady .... I met twenty years ago.

S	not omitted

205 Fill in : who, why, where, when, which, or whose.

Dear Mum and Dad,

Hi! Well here's my news. The day 1) ..*(when)*.. I arrived I felt very lonely. I am very happy now though, because the college 2) .... I am studying has a computer course. On Wednesday the boy 3) .... room I share had a party. It was great fun! Thursday was good. The man 4) .... teaches us Biology forgot to come so we had some free time! Friday wasn't so great. I missed a lecture. The reason 5) .... I missed it was that I was ill in bed. The photograph 6) .... I'm sending you was taken on the day 7) .... I arrived, while I was waiting for the bus. I'll have to catch up on my work, so I must go now! Write soon.   Love, Tom

14. Relatives

205 Join the sentences using who, when, where, which or whose.

1. She's the girl. She works in the library. *She's the girl who works in the library.*
2. Corfu is an island. It has many beautiful beaches. ....
3. Here's the alarm clock. I bought it yesterday. ....
4. I've spoken to John. His house was burgled last Monday. ....
5. That's the lady. Her jewellery was stolen. ....
6. That is the radio. I won it in the competition. ....
7. John is the man. His house was destroyed by the fire. ....
8. There is the hospital. I was born there. ....
9. That was the summer. I met my wife then. ....
10. That is Fiona Webb. She is a famous dancer. ....
11. Holland is the country. The best cheese is produced there. ....
12. 1945 was the year. The Second World War ended then. ....
13. That's the hotel. I stayed there last summer. ....
14. August is the month. Most people go on holiday then. ....

206 Complete the conversation using who, which, whose or where.

Simon : Hi Nigel! Where did you go on holiday?
Nigel : I went to Greece 1) ....*where*.... I had a nice time.
Simon : Did you see anything exciting?
Nigel : Yes. I went to the Acropolis, 2) .... is very famous. I also went to the place 3) .... the first Olympic Games were held.
Simon : Did you meet anyone interesting there?
Nigel : Yes, I met a girl 4) .... was from England. She knew a Greek family 5) .... lived in Athens and she took me to meet them. They were a very rich and kind family 6) .... friendliness made me feel very welcome.
Simon : It sounds like you enjoyed yourself!
Nigel : Yes, it's a place 7) .... I would like to go back to.

Defining / Non-defining relative clauses

A **defining relative clause** gives necessary information and is **essential** to the meaning of the main sentence. The clause is not put in commas. **Who, which** and **that** can be omitted when they are the object of the relative clause.
This is the book **(which) my friend wrote**. People **who smoke** damage their health.

A **non-defining relative clause** gives extra information and it is **not essential** to the meaning of the main sentence. In non-defining relative clauses the relative pronouns cannot be omitted. **That** cannot replace **who** or **which**. The clause is put in commas.
Mr Brown, **who lives next door**, went to Australia last week.

14. Relatives

208) Fill in the appropriate relative, say whether the relative clauses are essential or not to the meaning of the main sentence, then add commas where necessary.

1. Paul **, ..who...** is a famous actor **,** went to school with my brother.   ....not essential.....
2. The pen .... I left on that table has disappeared.   ....
3. The woman .... cleans our flat is very friendly.   ....
4. David .... grew up in Canada speaks fluent French.   ....
5. The man .... car was stolen has gone to the police station.   ....
6. Rye .... my grandmother lives is near the sea.   ....
7. Roger .... car has broken down is late for work.   ....
8. The Acropolis .... attracts many tourists is in Athens.   ....

209) Fill in the relative pronoun. Put commas where necessary. Write D for defining, ND for non-defining and if the relative can be omitted or not.

	ND	not omitted
1. Mr Brown **., who...** teaches us French **,** comes from London.		
2. The girl .... I met on the bus looks just like my sister.		
3. Peter Smith .... had an accident is in hospital.		
4. The apples .... grow on these trees are delicious.		
5. This apple pie .... I made yesterday tastes great.		
6. The film .... I saw on TV last night was very sad.		
7. My friend Alex .... is a doctor works very long hours.		
8. John .... father is a lawyer has moved to Paris.		
9. The sports centre .... we play tennis is expensive.		
10. The vase .... Mother gave me got broken.		
11. The summer .... I went to Spain I got really sunburnt.		
12. The car .... tyres are flat is mine.		
13. The café .... I first met my husband has closed down now.		
14. Simon .... mother is a vegetarian doesn't eat meat.		
15. The baker's .... is by my house sells wonderful pies.		

210) Match the phrases as in the example:

1. a blender	a path at the side of the road	you relax in it
2. a party	something	you mix things with it
3. an armchair	a machine	people walk along it
4. a pavement	a piece of furniture	people enjoy going to
5. a fork	an occasion	you eat with it

1. ..A blender is a machine you mix things with......
2. ....
3. ....
4. ....
5. ....

14. Relatives

211 Spot the mistakes and correct them.

The town 1) which I was born has changed greatly over the last fifty years. Now there is a modern shopping centre in the place 2) that my school used to be and all the children 3) whose went there have grown up and moved away. The local cinema, 4) that was built several years ago, used to be a dance hall 5) which big bands played. The park, 6) where was my favourite place as a child, is now a car park. Some things are still the same though. Mrs Jones, 7) whom is now seventy years old, still lives in the High Street and Mr Jones still owns the baker's shop, 8) that his two sons now work instead of him. The hospital 9) where I was born in is still standing, although it is now much bigger than it was at the time 10) which I was born. On the day 11) which my family and I left our home town we were all very sad.

1. *where*
2. ....
3. ....
4. ....
5. ....
6. ....
7. ....
8. ....
9. ....
10. ....
11. ....

Oral Activity 25

The teacher divides the class into two teams. The teams in turn choose word flashcards and make sentences using the correct relative pronoun/adverb. Each correct sentence gets 1 point. The team with the most points is the winner.

word flashcards : calendar/shows the date, watch/shows the time, teacher/teaches students, painter/paints pictures, park/go for walks, bus stop/wait for the bus etc.

Team A S1 : A calendar is something which shows the date.
Team B S1 : A watch is something which shows the time.   etc.

Writing Activity 17

Complete the following letter using relatives and any other necessary words as well as commas.

Dear John,

    We/move into/new house/last month. We/already meet/lot/people/neighbourhood. Ian/live/opposite us/be/doctor. His wife/children/be about same age/me/be/kind woman. Mr Brown/live/next door/have/dog/come into our garden/dig holes.

    The day/we move in/all neighbours/come/our house/welcome us/neighbourhood. Close/house/there be/park/we play football/other children/live/same street/us.

    Look forward/hear/you/soon.

Love, Ted

15. Reported Speech

Direct speech is the exact words someone said. We use quotation marks in Direct speech.

He said, "I'll wait for you."

Reported speech is the exact meaning of what someone said but not the exact words. We do not use quotation marks in Reported speech.

He said that he would wait for me.

Say – Tell

We use **say** in Direct speech. We also use **say** in Reported speech when **say** is not followed by the person the words were spoken to. We use **tell** in Reported speech when **tell** is followed by the person the words were spoken to.

Direct speech:	She **said to me**, "I am very tired."
Reported speech:	She **told me** that she was very tired.
Reported speech:	She **said that** she was very tired.

Expressions with say	say good morning etc, say something, say one's prayers, say so
Expressions with tell	tell the truth, tell a lie, tell a secret, tell a story, tell the time, tell the difference, tell sb one's name, tell sb the way, tell one from another

212 Fill in "say" or "tell" in the correct form.

1. The policeman …… *said* …… that the man was lying.
2. Philip ………………… it would probably rain tomorrow.
3. Susan …………………, "Let's go out for dinner tonight."
4. Jim ………………… me about the party last night.
5. Our teacher ………………… he was pleased with our work.
6. Yesterday my friend ………………… he ………………… (not) anyone my secret.

15. Reported Speech

7. Stop .... lies!
8. Could you please .... me your name?
9. The little girl .... her prayers and went to bed.
10. I really can't .... Jane from Kate. They are twins.
11. "I haven't got enough money," he .... to John.
12. He .... he would meet us later.

| We can report: | A. statements | B. questions | C. commands, requests, suggestions |

Reported Statements

1. **To report statements we use a reporting verb (say, tell, advise, explain, promise etc.) followed by a that-clause. In spoken English that may be omitted.**

2. **Pronouns and possessive adjectives change according to the meaning.**

   Direct speech : He said, "I can't fix it **myself**."
   Reported speech : He said **he** couldn't fix it **himself**.

3. **Certain words change as follows :**

   Direct speech :   this/these,   here,   come
   Reported speech :   that/those,   there,   go
                        "**This** is my book," he said.
                        He said **that** was his book.

   Note that :
   can changes to **could**
   will   "   " **would**
   may   "   " **might**
   must   "   " **had to**

114

15. Reported Speech

4. When the reporting verb is in the Past the verb tenses change as follows :

Direct speech	Reported speech
Present Simple "I **can't remember** his name," she said.	**Past Simple** She said she **couldn't remember** his name.
Present Continuous "She**'s speaking** to Joe," he said.	**Past Continuous** He said she **was speaking** to Joe.
Present Perfect "I**'ve bought** you some flowers," she said.	**Past Perfect** She said she **had bought** me some flowers.
Past Simple "He **lost** all the money," she said.	**Past Perfect** She said that he **had lost** all the money.
Future "I**'ll see** you later," he said.	**Conditional** He said he **would see** me later.

5. Time expressions change as follows :

Direct speech	Reported speech
tonight, today, this week/month/year now now that yesterday, last night/week/month/year tomorrow, next week/month/year two days/months/years etc., ago	that night, that day, that week/month/year then, at that time, at once, immediately since the day before, the previous night/week/month/year the day after, the following day, the next week/month/year two days/months/years etc., before
"He arrived **last week**," she said.	She said that he had arrived **the previous week.**

6. There are no changes in verb tenses when the reporting verb is in the Present, Future or Present Perfect tense or when the sentence expresses something which is always true.

Direct speech	She**'ll say**, "I can do it."	"The earth **is** round," said the teacher.
Reported speech	She**'ll say** (that) she can do it.	The teacher said (that) the earth **is** round.

7. The Past Continuous does not usually change.
  Direct speech :   "I **was travelling** to Brighton while she **was flying** to the USA," he said.
  Reported speech : He said he **was travelling** to Brighton while she **was flying** to the USA.

8. Certain modal verbs do not change in Reported speech. These are : **would**, **could**, **might**, **should**, **ought to**.

  Direct speech :   "He might visit us," Mum said.
  Reported speech : Mum said that he **might** visit us.

15. Reported Speech

213 Report what the guests said at a wedding last Sunday.

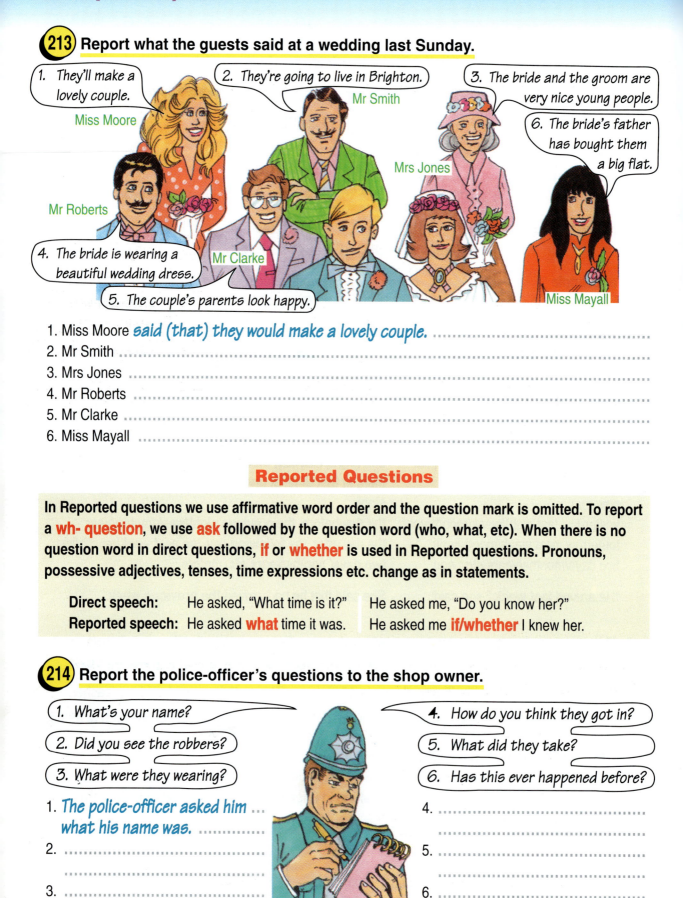

1. They'll make a lovely couple. — Miss Moore
2. They're going to live in Brighton. — Mr Smith
3. The bride and the groom are very nice young people. — Mrs Jones
4. The bride is wearing a beautiful wedding dress. — Mr Roberts
5. The couple's parents look happy. — Mr Clarke
6. The bride's father has bought them a big flat. — Miss Mayall

1. Miss Moore said (that) they would make a lovely couple.
2. Mr Smith
3. Mrs Jones
4. Mr Roberts
5. Mr Clarke
6. Miss Mayall

Reported Questions

In Reported questions we use affirmative word order and the question mark is omitted. To report a **wh- question**, we use **ask** followed by the question word (who, what, etc). When there is no question word in direct questions, **if** or **whether** is used in Reported questions. Pronouns, possessive adjectives, tenses, time expressions etc. change as in statements.

Direct speech: He asked, "What time is it?"   He asked me, "Do you know her?"
Reported speech: He asked **what** time it was.   He asked me **if/whether** I knew her.

214 Report the police-officer's questions to the shop owner.

1. What's your name?
2. Did you see the robbers?
3. What were they wearing?
4. How do you think they got in?
5. What did they take?
6. Has this ever happened before?

1. The police-officer asked him what his name was.
2.
3.
4.
5.
6.

15. Reported Speech

Reported Commands / Requests / Suggestions

To report commands, requests, suggestions etc we use a reporting verb (**order**, **ask**, **tell**, **advise**, **offer**, **warn**, **beg**, **suggest*** etc) followed by **to -infinitive** or **not to - infinitive**.
(***suggest** is followed by the **-ing form**. eg. He said, "Shall we go by bus?"   He suggested **going** by bus.)

| Direct speech: | He said to me, "Stop talking!" | He said to me, "Don't touch it!" |
| Reported speech: | He told me **to stop** talking. | He told me **not to touch** it. |

214 Report what Mrs Lane told her babysitter to do.

1. Don't answer the door to anyone!
2. Phone me if there's an emergency!
3. Don't let the children eat any sweets!
4. Send the children to bed at 9 o'clock!
5. Give the children a bath before they go to bed!
6. Don't take the dog into the children's bedroom!
7. Close all the windows!
8. Put the toys away in the cupboard!

1. Mrs Lane told her babysitter not to answer the door to anyone.
2.
3.
4.
5.
6.
7.
8.

215 Turn from Direct into Reported speech.

1. "I've ordered a pizza for dinner," he said. He said that he had ordered a pizza for dinner.
2. "We must write a letter to our lawyer," she said.

3. "I will come tomorrow and fix the tap," the plumber said to them.

4. "This is the best holiday I've ever had," she said to her friend.

5. "Why did you say that to me?" she asked him.
6. "Don't speak to your father like that," she said to them.

7. "Could you show me where the manager's office is?" he asked the secretary.

8. "Take your books with you," she said to her son.

117

15. Reported Speech

217 **Choose a reporting verb and turn the following from Direct into Reported speech.**

advised, asked, ordered, suggested, explained, warned, promised, begged, offered, refused

1. "I think you should take more exercise," the doctor said to me.
   The doctor advised me to take more exercise.
2. "I will not answer your questions," the actor said to him.
3. "I really will phone this evening," he said.
4. "Do you know where I've put my hat?" he said to her.
5. "What have you bought me for Christmas?" the little boy said to his parents.
6. "Go to your room now and do your homework," the mother said to her son.
7. "You will be paid twice a month," her boss said.
8. "Would you like me to drive you into town?" she said to me.
9. "Let's go for a walk!" he said.
10. "Please let me come with you," she said to her mother.
11. "Let's play in the garden," Ted said.
12. "The sun is bigger than the earth," Mary said to the children.
13. "Don't go near the fire because it's dangerous," she said to Ben.
14. "Let's have steak for dinner," said June.
15. "I promise I'll write to you as soon as I arrive, Mary," said John.
16. "Please, don't shoot me!" he said to the robber.

218 **First state if the following statements are true (T) or not true (NT) then turn them from Direct into Reported speech.**

1. "Penguins can swim," he said. ... *He said (that) penguins can swim.* — T
2. "The earth is flat," the old man said.
3. "The cheetah is the fastest animal in the world," she said.
4. "A train goes faster than a plane," he said.
5. "Dolphins are less intelligent than sharks," he said.
6. "Man does not live forever," she said.

15. Reported Speech

219 Write the exact words the customs officer asked Tracy.

The customs officer asked Tracy if she had got anything to declare. He asked her if she had bought anything in the Duty Free shop. He also asked her which hotel she was going to stay at. Then he asked her if she minded opening her suitcase. Next he asked her whose camera that was. He asked her if she was meeting anyone there. Finally he asked her what she had got in the bag and told her to have a pleasant stay.

1. Have you got anything to declare?
2. ...
3. ...
4. ...
5. ...
6. ...
7. ...
8. ...

220 Write the exact words Miss Prim said to her students.

Miss Prim told her students not to talk when she's talking. She told them to give their homework to her at the end of each lesson. She asked them not to write on the desks. Then she told them to put their hands up if they had a question. She also asked them not to eat in the classroom. She told them to write everything in pen and asked them to throw their rubbish into the wastepaper bin. Finally she told them not to leave the classroom without permission.

1. Don't talk when I'm talking!
2. ...
3. ...
4. ...
5. ...
6. ...
7. ...
8. ...

221 Turn the following dialogue into Reported Speech.

Sally: Have you applied for the job?
Diane: Yes, I had an interview yesterday.
Sally: How did it go?
Diane: Fine, but I'm wondering if I want the job because I will have to move to Manchester.
Sally: What will you do then?
Diane: If they offer me the job, I can't accept it.

Sally asked Diane if she had applied for the job. Diane told her ...

15. Reported Speech

221 Write what the family said at the dinner table.

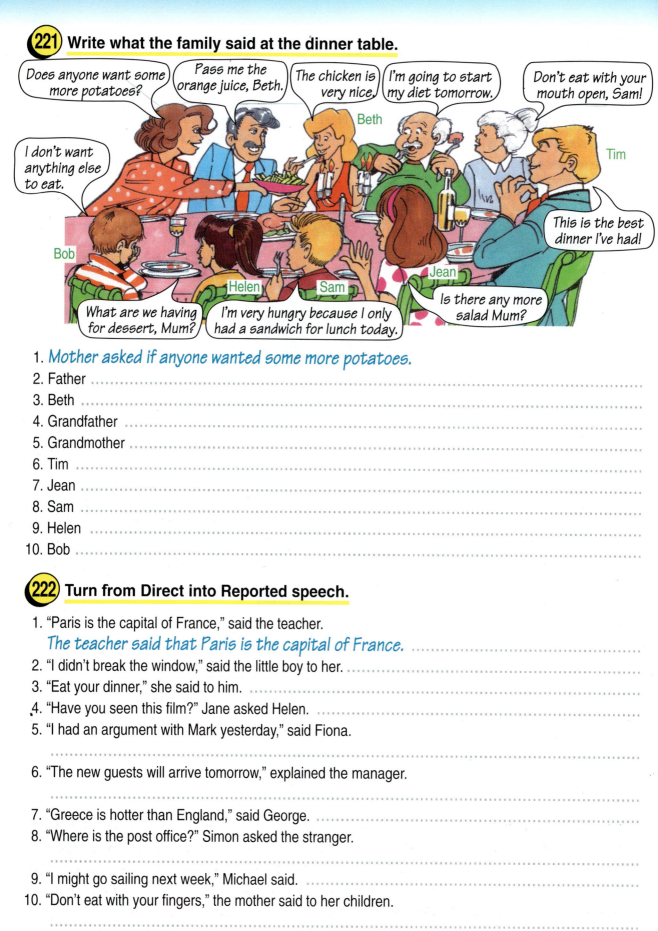

1. *Mother asked if anyone wanted some more potatoes.*
2. Father ....
3. Beth ....
4. Grandfather ....
5. Grandmother ....
6. Tim ....
7. Jean ....
8. Sam ....
9. Helen ....
10. Bob ....

222 Turn from Direct into Reported speech.

1. "Paris is the capital of France," said the teacher.
   The teacher said that Paris is the capital of France.
2. "I didn't break the window," said the little boy to her.
3. "Eat your dinner," she said to him.
4. "Have you seen this film?" Jane asked Helen.
5. "I had an argument with Mark yesterday," said Fiona.
6. "The new guests will arrive tomorrow," explained the manager.
7. "Greece is hotter than England," said George.
8. "Where is the post office?" Simon asked the stranger.
9. "I might go sailing next week," Michael said.
10. "Don't eat with your fingers," the mother said to her children.

15. Reported Speech

Oral Activity 26

The teacher divides the class into two teams. S1 from Team A whispers an untrue statement into S2's ear. S2 reports the statement to the class then he/she whispers another statement into S3's ear. When a student can't report a statement or think of a new one the team loses its turn. The team with the most correct sentences is the winner.

Team A S1: (whispers) I'm going on holiday next week.
Team A S2: He said he was going on holiday the next week.
(whispers) I have never eaten cheese.
Team A S3: She said she had never eaten cheese.
(whispers) I am 35 years old.
Team A S4: She said she is 35 years old.
Teacher : No! Team A loses its turn.

Oral Activity 27

The teacher chooses two students. One pretends to be a famous pop singer and the other a reporter who is hard of hearing. The rest of the class pretend to be reporters. The teacher gives the reporters word flashcards. They start asking the famous pop-singer questions and he/she answers. The deaf reporter asks, "What did he/she ask and what did he/she say?" The student who asked the question reports his/her question and the answer he/she got.

word flashcards : How old are you?, Where do you live?, Are you married?, Have you ever been to Madrid before?, Do you like Spanish food?, Are you staying here long?, Have you visited Toledo?, Who's your favourite actor?, Are you making a new LP?, Do you like sports cars?, Do you earn lots of money?, When did you start singing?, Do you write your own songs?, Are you going to try acting?, Do you work hard?, Can you fly a jet?, Do you play squash?, What's your favourite food?, Are you happy with your life?

e.g. S1: How old are you?
PS: I'm 25.
DR: What did you ask? What did she say?
S1: I asked how old she was and she said she was 25.

S2: Where do you live?
PS: I live in New York.
DR: What did you ask? What did she say?
S2: I asked where she lived and she said she lived in New York. etc.

Writing Activity 18

Detective Daniels is investigating a murder. Read what a suspect he questioned told him, then write the detective's report. "I have known James for many years. I have worked as his driver for ten years. I got on very well with him. I can't believe he is dead. The last time I saw him alive was at 10 o'clock last night. I drove him to the cinema in town and I left him there. On the way back I had a flat tyre. I think I arrived home at about 1 o'clock. You can check this information with my wife. I swear I didn't kill James!"

16. Prepositions of Place – Movement – Time

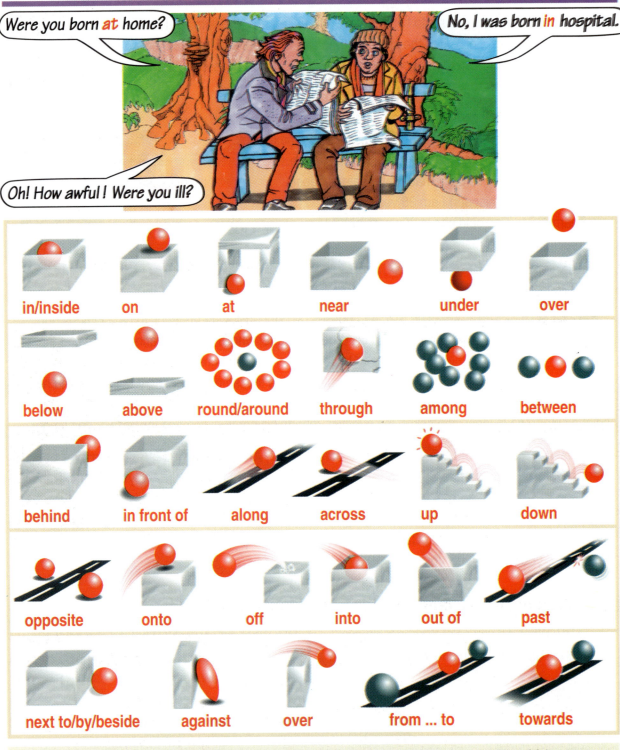

in +	cities / towns / streets / the suburbs / an armchair / danger / the middle of / the queue
at +	house number (at 23 Oxford St) / home / school / university / work / the bus-stop
on +	the floor / the outskirts / a chair / foot / holiday
by +	bus / taxi / car / helicopter / plane / train / coach / ship / boat / air / sea
BUT on	a / the bus / plane / train / coach / ship / boat – in a taxi / car / helicopter

16. Prepositions of Place - Movement - Time

224 Fill in: under, next to, in, on, onto, beside, in front of, over, near or behind.

Grandma is sitting 1) .... *under* ... the sunshade. Dad is sleeping 2) .... the sunbed. Tim is making sandcastles 3) .... Grandma. Ann is sitting 4) .... Tim. The dog is lying 5) .... Dad. Mum is waiting 6) .... the ice-cream stall. Jenny is hiding 7) .... the ice-cream stall. Peter is climbing 8) .... a stool. Sue and Bob are swimming 9) .... the sea. Some seagulls are flying 10) .... the sea.

225 Fill in: by, from...to, at, past, inside, out of, towards, across, against, under or through.

This is Newton High Street. An old lady is walking 1) ... *past* ... the post office. Her dog is looking at a cat which is hiding 2) .... a car. 3) .... the car there is a man. A woman is getting 4) .... the car. A policeman is walking 5) .... the street 6) .... the bank. A boy's bicycle is leaning 7) .... the lamp post. The boy is walking 8) .... the door of the sweet shop which is 9) .... the bank. There's a bus 10) .... the bus stop. It's going 11) .... Newton 12) .... Busworth.

226 Fill in: off, round, onto, out of, in, above, across or by.

A boy has just fallen 1) .... *off* .... his bicycle 2) .... the busy street. A young woman is running 3) .... the street to help him. The boy's books have fallen 4) .... his bag 5) .... the street and are lying all 6) .... him. His jacket is still 7) .... the bicycle basket. Two girls are standing 8) .... the post box watching the scene. 9) .... them there's an open window. An old woman is looking out to see what is happening.

16. Prepositions of Place - Movement - Time

227 Fill in: on, in, by or at.

Last year when I was 1) ...... *on* ...... holiday I received a telegram asking me to go home immediately. I travelled 2) .... plane and landed 3) .... London at midnight. My flight was terrible because there were lots of babies 4) .... the plane with me and most of them cried throughout the trip. After I left the airport, I waited 5) .... a bus stop for over half an hour but no bus came so I decided to continue my journey 6) .... taxi. My sister lives 7) .... 10, Mill Road, Hariton, and so I asked the driver to take me there. The house is 8) .... the outskirts of the town and it took quite a while to find. We had to stop 9) .... the suburbs to ask for directions as I had never been there before. When we finally arrived at the house, my sister was waiting for me.

228 Fill in: in front of, between, behind, under, past, towards, at, in or against.

There are lots of people 1) .. *In* .... the bank today. 2) .... the cashier's desk there's a long queue. Two cashiers are sitting 3) .... the desk. The manager is standing 4) .... the cashiers holding some papers. There's a guard 5) .... the door. He's leaning 6) .... the cashier's desk. He's got a gun 7) .... his arm. An old woman is going 8) .... the guard 9) .... the cashier. A man wearing a hat is standing 10) .... the queue 11) .... a couple.

229 Fill in: through, at, on, among, above, between, under, beside, near, in, against or in the middle of.

Mrs Moore is having a party this evening. She's standing 1) ... *among* ... her guests 2) .... the room pointing 3) .... a picture 4) .... the fireplace. There's a lot of food 5) .... the table and 6) .... the table there are several empty bottles. 7) .... the fireplace is the record player. A man is standing 8) .... it. A waitress is coming 9) .... the door holding a tray of drinks. A man is leaning 10) .... the wall 11) .... two women. They are holding glasses 12) .... their hands.

16. Prepositions of Place - Movement - Time

Prepositions of Time

AT	IN	ON
at 8:15	in the morning/afternoon/night	on Sunday
at Christmas/Easter	in July (months)	on Monday etc
at night/midnight/noon	in summer (seasons)	on March 28th
at the weekend	in 1991 (years)	on a winter night
	in the 20th century	

Note: **on time** = at the right time **at 8:30** = exactly at that time
 in time = early enough, not late **by 8:30** = not later than that time, before

 229 Fill in : at, in or on.

1. ...*in*... the evening
2. .... Monday
3. .... midnight
4. .... April 13th
5. .... 5.30
6. .... Tuesday morning
7. .... Christmas
8. .... 6.30
9. .... November
10. .... the summer
11. 1967
12. .... noon
13. .... the 15th century
14. .... Sunday morning
15. .... a spring night

230 Fill in: in, on or at.

My birthday is 1) ....*on*...... the 30th of July. Last year I had a great day. I got up 2) .... 8 o'clock 3) .... the morning and tidied the house. Then 4) .... the afternoon I went into town with my friend to buy food for the party. The party started 5) .... 7 o'clock 6) .... the evening and didn't stop until very late 7) .... night! 8) .... the 31st of July I was very tired, so I went to bed early 9) .... the evening.

231 Fill in: in, opposite, through, out of, to, inside, into, round, on or above.

There are lots of people 1) ..*in/inside*.... the "Copper Key" restaurant this evening. 2) .... each table there's a candle and a vase of flowers. There are chairs 3) .... the tables and a fireplace 4) .... the door. 5) .... the fireplace there's a nice painting. A waiter is coming 6) .... the kitchen carrying a tray of food. Another waiter is pouring juice 7) .... the glasses. A couple has just come 8) .... the restaurant 9) .... the door. The manager is showing them 10) .... their table.

16. Prepositions of Place - Movement - Time

233 Fill in: at, in, by or on.

Last year 1) **at** Easter I went to England for a short holiday. I arrived in London 2) .... Friday 3) .... 11 o'clock 4) .... the evening. I went to my hotel by taxi, which got me there in about an hour. I was so tired by then that I went straight to bed. When I woke up 5) .... the morning I remembered that I had made an appointment to meet a friend 6) .... 10:30. I thought I could never get ready 7) .... time, but in the end I had reached the café 8) .... 10.15. My friend arrived 9) .... time. 10) .... 1 o'clock we went to a restaurant for lunch and 11) .... the afternoon we went to a museum.

234 Fill in: over, round, into, down, on, up, along, out of or towards.

Today is Christmas Eve. The centre of town is very busy. Lots of people are going 1) **into** and 2) .... the shops buying Christmas presents. They are walking 3) .... and 4) .... the street looking in the windows. There are some children dancing and singing carols 5) .... the Christmas tree. A car is coming 6) .... the corner. It has a Christmas tree 7) .... the roof. A man is going to put some parcels 8) .... his car. His wife is coming 9) .... the street 10) .... him with more parcels. There are Christmas decorations hanging 11) .... the street.

235 Fill in: at, on or in.

Hightown Zoo opens 1) **at** 9 o'clock 2) .... the morning. 3) .... Saturdays and Sundays it opens 4) .... 10.30. It's a good idea to come early 5) .... the summer because the zoo gets very full. The best time to visit is 6) .... the afternoon because you can see the animals being fed. The zoo first opened 7) .... Easter 8) .... 1903. But most of the buildings were built 9) .... the nineteenth century. People can visit Hightown Zoo 10) .... any time, 11) .... summer or 12) .... winter. It's only closed 13) .... Christmas and 14) .... 1st January.

236 Fill in: at, to, by, or in.

Last summer, 1) **at** the end of July, I went 2) .... Nottingham to visit a friend who was 3) .... university there. I arrived 4) .... the afternoon and went 5) .... bus to my friend's house, which is 6) .... the suburbs of the town, 7) .... 123, Park Manor Road. My friend wasn't 8) ...... home, so I waited until she got back 9) .... 5 o'clock. 10) .... the evening we went out to have a drink 11) ...... the oldest pub 12) .... England, which was built 13) .... the 13th century.

16. Prepositions of Place - Movement - Time

 236 Fill in : on, at, opposite, beside, in, behind, under, over or below.

John works 1) .. *at/in* . a film studio. He is a cameraman. He is sitting 2) .... his camera 3) .... a big light. Standing 4) .... John is a man holding a microphone. He is recording the actors. The woman 5) .... the ladder is repairing a light. She has a bag of tools 6) .... her shoulder. There are two actors 7) .... the studio. They are standing 8) .... each other with swords in their hands. 9) .... them there is a gate and a wall. A woman is sitting 10) .... a big chair. She is holding a megaphone 11) .... her hand and shouting at the actors. She is the director of the film.

Oral Activity 28

The teacher divides the class into two teams and asks them to look at the picture for Ex. 237 for 2 minutes. Then the students close their books and answer the teacher's questions in turn. Each correct answer gets 1 point. The team with the most points is the winner.

Teacher:	Where does John work?	Team BS1:	In front of a camera.
Team AS1:	In a film studio.	Teacher:	No! Behind his camera.
Teacher:	Where is he standing?		Team B doesn't get a point.

Oral Activity 29

The teacher divides the class into two teams. Then he/she says expressions of time without their prepositions. The teams in turn give the missing preposition. Each correct answer gets 1 point. The team with the most points is the winner.

Teacher:	summer	Teacher:	Monday afternoon
Team AS1:	in summer	Team BS1:	on Monday afternoon etc.

Writing Activity 19

Find a magazine picture and describe the position of the people and things in it. (60 - 80 words)

17. Articles

17. Articles

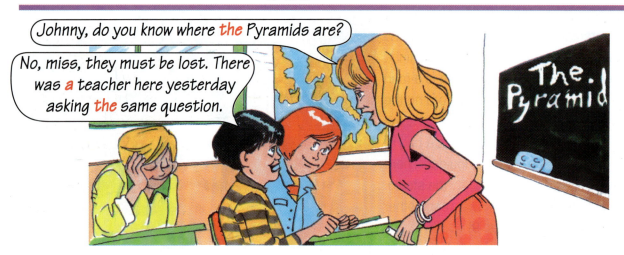

1. **A/An** is used with **singular countable** nouns when we talk about things **in general**.
   An aeroplane is faster than **a** train.   **A** greengrocer sells vegetables.
   (Which aeroplane? Aeroplanes in general.)   (Which greengrocer? Greengrocers in general.)

2. We often use **a/an** after the verbs **to be** and **to have**.
   He **is** a photographer. He **has got** a camera.

3. We do not use **a/an** with **uncountable** or **plural** nouns. We can use **some** instead.
   Would you like **some** tea? Yes, please! And I'd like **some** biscuits.

4. **The** is used before **singular** and **plural** nouns, both **countable** and **uncountable** when we are talking about something **specific** or when the noun is mentioned **for a second time**.
   The boy who has just left is my cousin. (Which boy? Not any boy. The specific boy, the boy who has just left.)
   There is a cat on the sofa. **The** cat is sleeping. ("The cat" is mentioned for a second time.)

5. We use **the** with the words **cinema, theatre, radio, country(side), seaside, beach, etc**.
   We go to **the beach** every Sunday.

6. We use both **a/an** or **the** before a singular countable noun to represent a **class** of people, animals or things.
   A/The dolphin is more intelligent than **a/the** shark. (We mean dolphins and sharks in general.)
   ALSO: Dolphins are more intelligent than sharks.

237 Fill in: a, an or the.

Last night I went to 1) ..**an**.. Indonesian restaurant. I had 2) ..a.. very nice meal with 3) ..a.. good friend, Helen. 4) ..The.. waiter was Chinese. 5) ..The.. food was great. We drank 6) ..a.. bottle of Coke. When we asked for 7) ..the.. bill we didn't have enough money, so we had to do 8) ..the.. washing-up. It was not 9) ..a.. good way to end 10) ..the.. evening.

17. Articles

238 Fill in: a, an or the.

I arrived at 1) ..*the*.. airport just in time to see 2) ..*an*.. aeroplane take off. There is nothing unusual about this, except that I was supposed to be on that plane! When I went to 3) ..*the*.. desk to ask when 4) ..*the*.. next available flight was, I heard 5) ..*an*.. awful noise. I turned to see 6) ..*a*.. car crashing through 7) ..*the*.. front windows with 8) ..*a*.. police car just behind it. As I ran towards 9) ..*the*.. departure gate 10) ..*a*.. policeman stopped me to see if I was 11) ..*the*.. armed robber they were chasing. I told him I was not 12) ..*an*.. armed robber but 13) ..*a*.. businessman who had missed his plane. He let me go and I was able to catch 14) ..*the*.. last flight to my destination.

The is also used before :	The is omitted before :
1. **nouns which are unique.** Haven't you been to **the Acropolis** yet?	1. **proper nouns.** **Paula** comes from **Canada**.
2. **names of cinemas** (the Odeon), **hotels** (the Hilton), **theatres** (the Rex), **museums** (the Prado), **newspapers** (the Times), **ships** (the Queen Mary).	2. **names of sports, activities, colours, substances and meals.** He plays **tennis** well. She likes **blue. Coke** isn't expensive. **Lunch** is ready.
3. **names of rivers** (the Thames), **seas** (the Black Sea), **groups of islands/states** (the Bahamas, the USA), **mountain ranges** (the Alps), **deserts** (the Gobi desert), **oceans** (the Pacific) **and names with ... of** (The Tower of London).	3. **names of countries** (England), **cities** (London), **streets** (Bond Street), **parks** (Hyde Park), **mountains** (Everest), **islands** (Cyprus), **lakes** (Lake Michigan), **continents** (Europe).
4. **musical instruments.** Can you play **the guitar**?	4. **the poss/ve case or poss/ve adjectives.** This isn't **your** coat, it's **Kate's**.
5. **names of people / families / nationalities in the plural.** the Smiths, the English, the Dutch etc.	5. **the words "home" and "Father/Mother"** when we talk about our own home/parents. **Father** isn't at **home**.
6. **titles without proper names.** the Queen, the President	6. **titles with proper names.** Queen Elizabeth, President Kennedy
7. **adjectives used as plural nouns** (the rich) **and the superlative degree of adjectives / adverbs** (the best). He's **the most intelligent** student of all.	7. **bed, school, church, hospital, prison,** when they are used for the reason they exist. John was sent to **prison. BUT** : His mother went to **the prison** to visit him last week.

17. Articles

240 Fill in "the" where necessary.

1. Is ..X.. Lisbon ..the.. capital of ..X.. Portugal?
2. Is ——— Malta in .the. Mediterranean?
3. Is ——— Paris in .the. United Kingdom or in .the. France?
4. Where is .the. Sahara Desert?
5. What is .the. biggest island in ——— Greece?
6. What is .the. capital of ——— Italy?
7. Is .the. Indian Ocean bigger than .the. Arctic Ocean?
8. Is ——— Everest the highest mountain in .the. world?
9. Where are ——— Malta and ——— Corsica?
10. Where are .the. Mississippi River and .the. Thames?

241 Fill in: a, an or the.

At 1) ..the... weekend, Alex and Amanda went to 2) .the. theatre. They saw 3) .a. great play called "I Would Die For You". 4) .The. play was 5) .a. romantic story about 6) .the. lives of 7) .a. couple in love. After going to 8) .the. theatre, Alex and Amanda went to 9) .a. restaurant. They both ate 10) .a. very large meal. Amanda had 11) .a. huge bowl of spaghetti and Alex had 12) .an. enormous plate of various kinds of meat. 13) .The. spaghetti and meat were followed by chocolate cake. After leaving 14) .the. restaurant, Alex and Amanda got 15) .a. taxi home. On the way home they saw 16) .a. nasty car accident. 17) .A. yellow car had run straight into 18) .a. black van. 19) .The. yellow car was badly damaged. 20) .The. taxi driver had to take Alex and Amanda home by another route.

242 Fill in "a" or "the" where necessary.

Last year 1) .. the ... Smiths went on holiday to 2) ——— London with their friends 3) .the. Browns. They visited 4) ——— Hyde Park and went on 5) .a. boat trip on 6) .The. Thames. 7) ——— Mrs Brown visited 8) ——— Buckingham Palace hoping to see 9) .The. Queen. Unfortunately, 10) ——— Queen Elizabeth II wasn't at 11) ——— home at the time.

243 Fill in "a", "an" or "the" where necessary.

1. Is ..a... tomato ..a... fruit or ..a.. vegetable?
2. Is .an. apple ——— red or ——— blue?
3. What is .the. capital of ——— France?

17. Articles

4. When we visited — London we stayed at *the* Hilton Hotel.
5. Does *the* River Seine run through — Paris or — Madrid?
6. Is *the* Indian Ocean larger than *the* Mediterranean Sea?
7. Is — New York in *the* USA or in — Canada?
8. Is *an/the* elephant bigger than *an/the* alligator?
9. Does *the* Amazon run through — Africa or — South America?

244 Fill in "a" or "the" where necessary.

John : Do you want to come to 1) *the* theatre with me tonight?
Ann : Sorry, I can't. I'm going to 2) *a* restaurant with my cousin from 3) — America.
John : What part of 4) *the* USA does he come from?
Ann : He lives in 5) — Colorado, near 6) *the* Rocky Mountains. He's quite 7) *a* famous man in America. He plays 8) *the* guitar in 9) *a* rock band. In fact he's giving a concert at 10) *The* Odeon in 11) — Regent Street tomorrow evening.

245 Fill in: a, an or the.

A: Oh, 1) *a* glove! Where's that from?
B: It's 2) *the* glove Michael Jackson wore in the "Bad" video!
A: Why's there 3) *a* can of Pepsi here?
B: Oh, that's 4) *the* can that Michael drank from in the Pepsi advertisement.
A: Oh and 5) *an* old pair of flared trousers. They're horrible.
B: They're my prize possession. Those are 6) *the* trousers he wore when he was with the Jackson Five!
A: Oh and let me guess, this was one of 7) *the* bananas Bubbles ate!
B: No, don't be stupid, that was my breakfast!

246 Fill in "an" or "the" where necessary.

1) *X* Australia is 2) *an* interesting country. 3) *The* Australians are very friendly, happy people. Some of 4) *the* strangest animals in 5) *the* world live there. In 6) *the* Great Victoria Desert you can find 7) — kangaroos and 8) — koala bears. 9) *The* most famous city in Australia is 10) — Sydney.

Oral Activity 30

The teacher divides the class into two teams. Then he/she says words and teams in turn add "the" where necessary. Each correct answer gets 1 point. The team with the most points is the winner.

Teacher:	Taj Mahal	Teacher:	Aegean Sea
Team AS1:	the Taj Mahal	Team AS2:	Aegean Sea
Teacher:	Alps	Teacher:	No! the Aegean Sea.
Team BS1:	the Alps	Team A doesn't get a point.	

18. Wishes

	Form	Use
I wish (if only) (wish about the present)	+ **Past Simple** I wish he **were/was** with us now.	We express a wish about a present situation which we want to be different.
I wish (if only) (wish about the present)	+ **subject** + **could** + **bare infinitive** I wish he **could** learn faster.	We use this pattern for a wish or regret in the present concerning lack of ability.
I wish (if only) (wish about the future)	+ **subject** + **would** + **bare infinitive** (we never say : I wish I would) I wish he **would stop** drinking so much.	We express a wish for a change in the future.
I wish (if only) (regret about the past)	+ **Past Perfect** I wish he **hadn't failed** his test.	We express a regret or a wish that something happened or didn't happen in the past.

1. "**If only**" means the same as "**I wish**" but it is more emphatic.
   I **wish** he could help me. **If only** he could help me. (stronger, more emphatic)

2. After "**I wish**" we may use "**were**" instead of "**was**" in all persons.
   I wish I **was/were** rich.

18. Wishes

246 Ann doesn't like her new house. Write what she wishes.

The house is so old and dirty. She has to paint it. The house doesn't have central heating. The kitchen is small.

1. I wish the house wasn't so old and dirty.
2. ....
3. ....
4. ....

247 Kate wants things to be different in the future. Write what she wishes.

I want my father to give me more pocket money. I want my brothers to stop fighting. I don't want my mother to make me eat vegetables. I don't want my sister to wear my clothes.

1. I wish my father would give me more pocket money.
2. ....
3. ....
4. ....

248 Ted regrets what he did or didn't do. Write what he wishes.

He left his job. He didn't listen to his wife. He robbed a bank. He was sent to prison.

1. I wish I hadn't left my job.
2. ....
3. ....
4. ....

249 Fill in: wish about the present, regret about the past, wish about the future; then write what the people wish.

1. regret about the past

   I wish I hadn't eaten too many cakes.

   He ate too many cakes.

2. ....

   He is not good-looking.

3. ....

   She broke her leg.

18. Wishes

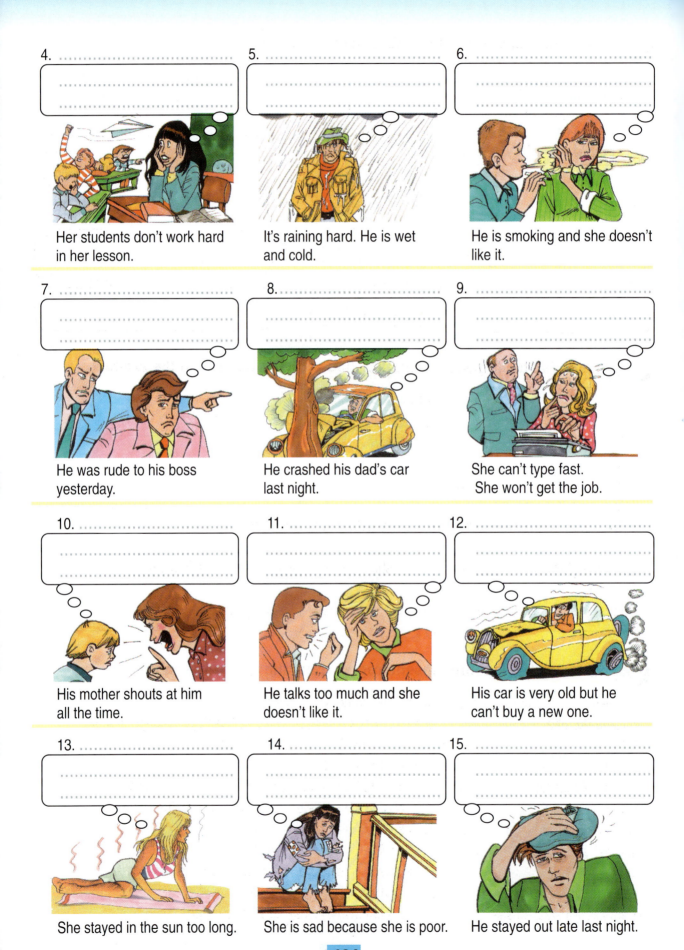

18. Wishes

251 **Read what Hilda says and write what she wishes.**

I didn't go to university. I didn't get any qualifications. I can't find a better job. The telephone never stops ringing. My boss doesn't like me. I'd like to be rich. I always feel tired. It was wrong of me to shout at Ann.

1. *I wish I had gone to university.*
2.
3.
4.
5.
6.
7.
8.

252 **Write what these people wish they had or hadn't done as in the example:**

1. John drove his car so fast that he had an accident.
   John: *I wish I hadn't driven my car so fast. I wouldn't have had an accident.*
2. Julie was late and she missed the beginning of the film.
   Julie:
3. Jack ate too much and he was sick.
   Jack:
4. Claire was very nervous during her driving test and she didn't pass.
   Claire:
5. Susan didn't take off her gold ring when she went swimming and she lost it in the sea.
   Susan:
6. Terry and Jane didn't save any money so they didn't go on holiday last summer.
   Terry and Jane:

253 **Fill in the correct form of the verbs in brackets.**

1. I wish I *had met* (meet) that actor when he was in town.
2. He wishes he .... (buy) that book last week - now he hasn't got enough money.
3. If only I .... (be) older, I could have a driving licence.
4. I wish I .... (can) remember where that book is.
5. Tony wishes he .... (go) to Paris with his brother, but he has to work.
6. If only the dog .... (not/eat) the tickets - now we can't go to the show.
7. If only I .... (not/make) that mistake yesterday.
8. I wish this box .... (not/be) so heavy - I can't lift it.
9. We wish we .... (not/leave) the gate open. Now the dog has escaped.
10. Paula wishes she .... (have) more time for gardening, but she hasn't.
11. Mrs Brown wishes she .... (write) those letters yesterday.

18. Wishes

254 Using the bold type in the sentences, write wishes as in the example:

1. **You left the radio on** and now the batteries don't work.
   You say, "*..I wish I hadn't left the radio on..* ...."
2. It's very dark outside and **you can't find your torch**.
   You say, ".."
3. **You didn't do your homework** and your teacher is angry.
   You say, ".."
4. You are looking at a beautiful flower. **You don't know what it is called**.
   You say, ".."
5. It's raining outside and **you want it to stop**.
   You say, ".."
6. **You stayed up late last night** and today you're very tired.
   You say, ".."
7. You are having a party **but nobody has come yet**.
   You say, ".."
8. You have short, straight hair. **You would like long, curly hair**.
   You say, ".."
9. You have just left your house and **left the keys inside**.
   You say, ".."
10. It is Christmas Day and **it doesn't look like it is going to snow**.
    You say, ".."
11. You live in the city. **You prefer the countryside**.
    You say, ".."

Oral Activity 31

The teacher divides the class into two teams. Then he/she pretends to be a magic genie. The teams in turn make wishes. Each grammatically correct sentence gets 1 point. The team with the most points is the winner.

Team AS1:   I wish I had a lot of money.
Team BS1:   I wish I were taller.
Team AS2:   I wish I am famous.
Teacher: No! I wish I **was/were** famous.
             Team A doesn't get a point.

Oral Activity 32

The teacher divides the class into two teams. The teams in turn make sentences about what an unhappy housewife wishes to change in her life in the future. Each grammatically correct sentence gets 1 point. The team with the most points is the winner.

Team AS1:   I wish my children would get better marks.
Team BS1:   I wish my husband would come home earlier.   etc.

Revision Exercises IV

Oral Activity 33

The teacher divides the class into two teams. Then he/she hands out flashcards to the students with situations on them. The students in turn make sentences expressing regrets in the past for each situation. Each grammatically correct sentence gets 1 point. The team with the most points is the winner.

word flashcards: feel tired, have stomach-ache, have a headache, have a cold, feel depressed, feel sick, feel hot, have toothache, have a sore throat, have sore feet, etc.

Team A S1 (feel tired): I wish I had slept more.
Team B S1 (have stomach-ache): I wish I hadn't eaten so much last night. etc.

Writing Activity 20

Read the following letter then rewrite it using wishes.

Dear Sarah,
I am having a terrible holiday. I shouldn't have chosen to stay on this island; I should have gone to Greece instead. The weather is awful. Yesterday it even rained! I really want to get a suntan but it's not possible because the sun never comes out. The hotel isn't very nice either and the staff are very impolite. I would like to complain to the manager but he is never here. I really miss my friends and my family and I feel like going home tomorrow!
Yours,
Nicky

 # Revision Exercises IV

255) Find the mistake and correct it.

1. It's hot in here. I think I'm going to open the window. ..... I'll .....
2. Martha feeds the baby when I arrived at her house.
3. He told, "I'm tired."
4. Simon plays the piano well, can't he?
5. He would like going to Madrid when he finishes university.
6. I'll leave the office when I will finish.
7. She hasn't met him for last year.
8. You mustn't make the beds. I've just made them.
9. By the time the police arrived the burglars escaped.
10. Both of them is from London.

Revision Exercises IV

255 Rewrite the sentences using the words given in bold type.

1. I don't think he's rich.
   CAN'T ...He can't be rich.
2. It isn't necessary for you to take a jacket.
   NEED ....
3. Shall I help you with your luggage?
   WOULD ....
4. I advise you to see a dentist.
   OUGHT ....
5. It's just possible that he'll phone tonight.
   MAY ....
6. You are not allowed to talk during the exam.
   MUSTN'T ....
7. They don't have to go to the meeting this evening.
   NEEDN'T ....

256 Add questions and short answers as in the example:

1. Colin has gone on holiday, ...hasn't he...? Yes, ...he has...
2. He went to Florida, ...? No, ... He went to Spain.
3. He can speak English, ...? Yes, ...
4. Florida's very hot at this time of year, ...? Yes, ...
5. He'll be back on Wednesday, ...? No, ... He'll be back in three weeks.

257 Turn from Active into Passive.

1. Professor Hoskins taught my brother. ...My brother was taught by Professor Hoskins.
2. David is going to paint the kitchen.
3. Someone had set the building on fire.
4. You haven't fixed the tap.
5. People should throw litter into the bin.
6. Her boyfriend gave her a diamond ring.
7. Is he repairing Mr Smith's car?
8. Calvin Klein designed her dress.

258 Fill in the, a or an where necessary.

Socrates was 1) ..an.. ancient Greek philosopher. He was born in 2) ...... Athens, 3) ...... son of 4) ...... sculptor, in 5) ...... year 470 B.C. He fought as 6) ...... soldier in 7) ...... Peloponnesian War. Socrates married 8) ...... woman whose name was Xanthippe. 9) ...... woman had 10) ...... very bad temper. Socrates was accused of setting 11) ...... bad example to 12) ...... youth of 13) ...... Athens and was sent to 14) ...... prison. He died by taking 15) ...... poison.

259 Put the verbs in brackets into the correct tense.

1. If she ..hurries............ (hurry), she'll be in time for the meeting.
2. If he .... (not/eat) so much, he wouldn't have felt so ill.
3. If you .... (go) to the market, will you get me some fruit?

4. If you washed the car, it .... (look) much better.
5. They .... (ring) us if they had been in town.

261 Fill in : next to, beside, between, behind, across, in, over, along, on or under.

Michael is fishing 1) ...*beside*... the river. Michael's dog is lying 2) .... him. His friend Jenny is standing 3) .... a tree. There is a boat 4) .... the bridge and a man 5) .... the boat. He is fishing too. There is a man riding his motorbike 6) .... the road. A man is driving a car 7) .... the bridge. There is a man 8) .... the motorbike. He is walking 9) .... the road. There are some birds flying 10) .... the river and there is a girl lying 11) .... the grass 12) .... two trees.

262 Write questions to which the words in bold type are the answers.

Peter went on a school trip **to Paris**. He went there **last summer**. He stayed there **for five days**. He was **with his class**. They had a fantastic time. They saw **the Mona Lisa**. This painting is in **the Louvre**. They also climbed up to **the top of the Eiffel Tower**. Peter had **never** been abroad before. He's planning to go to Paris again **next year**. He likes **Paris** very much.

1. ...*Where did Peter go*........................ ?   6. .... ?
2. .... ?   7. .... ?
3. .... ?   8. .... ?
4. .... ?   9. .... ?
5. .... ?   10. .... ?

263 Rewrite the following passage in the Passive Voice.

Someone broke into the National Museum last night. He broke down the door. He stole some valuable paintings and he destroyed a statue. The police have found fingerprints on the walls. They hope they will catch the thief soon.

....
....

264 Fill in the blanks using Past Simple or Present Perfect Simple or Continuous.

Tony Williams 1) ...*has been working*.... (work) for "Music News" for seven years now, and he loves his job. He 2) .... (start) there as a messenger boy when he was sixteen and he 3) .... (become) a reporter after two years. Since then he 4) .... (interview) many famous stars and he 5) .... (write) hundreds of articles. For the past hour and a half he 6) .... (talk) to Tanya Tanner, the beautiful singer and actress, but he 7) .... (not/finish) the interview yet because he finds her very interesting.

Revision Exercises IV

264 Fill in the blanks using the appropriate tense.

Milton Jackson is a Jamaican who 1) ..*lives*.. (live) in Manchester. He 2) .... (leave) his home in Kingston when he was eighteen years old. He 3) .... (work) in a bar there for four years when he 4) .... (decide) to go to England to look for a better job. So he 5) .... (buy) a one-way boat ticket to Liverpool. While he 6) .... (sunbathe) on the deck he 7) .... (meet) an Englishwoman called Kate who 8) .... (be) on holiday in Jamaica. "You must come and visit me in Manchester," she 9) .... (say). "I 10) .... (introduce) you to my brother. He's a footballer." "Who 11) .... (he/play) for?" 12) .... (ask) Milton. "Manchester United. He 13) .... (play) for them for two years now." Milton was very excited. He 14) .... (play) football since he was a young boy. As soon as they 15) .... (arrive) in England, Milton 16) .... (go) to Manchester with his new friend and met her brother, who 17) .... (introduce) him to the team manager. Now, he 18) .... (play) for Manchester United every week and at the moment he 19) .... (have) the time of his life. He 20) .... (already/travel) all over Europe and he 21) .... (make) lots of friends. He 22) .... (own) a big house in Cheshire and 23) .... (drive) a Porsche. What about Kate? Well, she and Milton 24) .... (get) married sometime next August.

265 Fill in with the correct form of the verbs in brackets.

One rainy Saturday it was too wet 1) ..*to go*... (go) outside so I decided 2) .... (spend) the day clearing out the attic. I was busy 3) .... (clear) away some papers when I noticed something which made me 4) .... (stop) what I was doing. It was a dusty old diary. Without 5) .... (hesitate), I opened it and was surprised 6) .... (see) it had belonged to my grandmother, now dead. I spent the rest of the afternoon 7) .... (read) it and was surprised 8) .... (learn) many interesting things about her past. I knew it would be worth 9) .... (have) it published. I was right, and I have only one regret; I wish my grandmother could 10) .... (be) here to enjoy the fame.

266 Read what the poor man is saying and write what he wishes.

I've always wanted to travel to Bali. I don't have much money. I've lost my job. I can't find another job. I smoke a lot. I don't have any friends. I'm poor. I didn't finish school.

1. ..*I wish I could travel to Bali.*..
2. ....
3. ....
4. ....
5. ....
6. ....
7. ....
8. ....

Revision Exercises IV

267 Write what the people said.

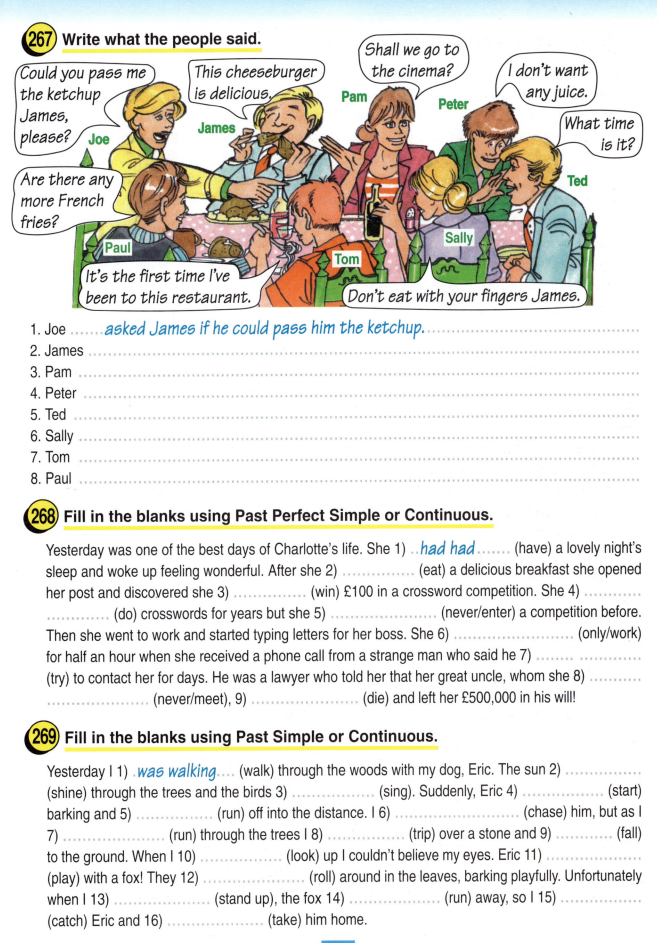

1. Joe ...... *asked James if he could pass him the ketchup.* ......
2. James ....
3. Pam ....
4. Peter ....
5. Ted ....
6. Sally ....
7. Tom ....
8. Paul ....

268 Fill in the blanks using Past Perfect Simple or Continuous.

Yesterday was one of the best days of Charlotte's life. She 1) *had had* (have) a lovely night's sleep and woke up feeling wonderful. After she 2) .... (eat) a delicious breakfast she opened her post and discovered she 3) .... (win) £100 in a crossword competition. She 4) .... (do) crosswords for years but she 5) .... (never/enter) a competition before. Then she went to work and started typing letters for her boss. She 6) .... (only/work) for half an hour when she received a phone call from a strange man who said he 7) .... (try) to contact her for days. He was a lawyer who told her that her great uncle, whom she 8) .... (never/meet), 9) .... (die) and left her £500,000 in his will!

269 Fill in the blanks using Past Simple or Continuous.

Yesterday I 1) *was walking* (walk) through the woods with my dog, Eric. The sun 2) .... (shine) through the trees and the birds 3) .... (sing). Suddenly, Eric 4) .... (start) barking and 5) .... (run) off into the distance. I 6) .... (chase) him, but as I 7) .... (run) through the trees I 8) .... (trip) over a stone and 9) .... (fall) to the ground. When I 10) .... (look) up I couldn't believe my eyes. Eric 11) .... (play) with a fox! They 12) .... (roll) around in the leaves, barking playfully. Unfortunately when I 13) .... (stand up), the fox 14) .... (run) away, so I 15) .... (catch) Eric and 16) .... (take) him home.

Summary of Tenses

271 Fill in the blanks using who, which or where.

Egypt, 1) ....*which*..... is situated in north-east Africa, is a country 2) .... you can find many interesting things. In ancient times the Pharaohs, 3) .... were regarded as gods, were buried in the pyramids. These are huge stone structures 4) .... took hundreds of years to build. The workers 5) .... started to build them never saw them finished. Each pyramid contains many rooms, the most important of 6) .... is the burial chamber, 7) .... the body of the Pharaoh was kept. It is said that anyone 8) .... enters this room will have bad luck for the rest of his life. But the great Pyramids are not the only things 9) .... attract people to Egypt. The Sphinx, 10) .... is situated near the Pyramid of Khafre, is a huge dog-like statue. It was meant to guard the tombs from anyone 11) .... may have tried to rob them.

Summary of Tenses

The Verb "to be"

Affirmative	Negative	Interrogative
I am	I'm not	Am I?
You are	You aren't	Are you?
He is	He isn't	Is he?
She is	She isn't	Is she?
It is	It isn't	Is it?
We are	We aren't	Are we?
You are	You aren't	Are you?
They are	They aren't	Are they?

Past tense "to be"

Affirmative	Negative	Interrogative
I was	I wasn't	Was I?
You were	You weren't	Were you?
He was	He wasn't	Was he?
She was	She wasn't	Was she?
It was	It wasn't	Was it?
We were	We weren't	Were we?
You were	You weren't	Were you?
They were	They weren't	Were they?

The Verb "to have"

Affirmative	Negative	Interrogative
I have got	I haven't (got)	Have I got?
You have got	You haven't (got)	Have you got?
He has got	He hasn't (got)	Has he got?
She has got	She hasn't (got)	Has she got?
It has got	It hasn't (got)	Has it got?
We have got	We haven't (got)	Have we got?
You have got	You haven't (got)	Have you got?
They have got	They haven't (got)	Have they got?

Past tense "to have"

Affirmative	Negative	Interrogative
I had	I didn't have	Did I have?
You had	You didn't have	Did you have?
He had	He didn't have	Did he have?
She had	She didn't have	Did she have?
It had	It didn't have	Did it have?
We had	We didn't have	Did we have?
You had	You didn't have	Did you have?
They had	They didn't have	Did they have?

The Verb "can"

Affirmative	Negative	Interrogative
I can	I can't	Can I?
You can	You can't	Can you?
He can	He can't	Can he?
She can	She can't	Can she?
It can	It can't	Can it?
We can	We can't	Can we?
You can	You can't	Can you?
They can	They can't	Can they?

Past tense "Can"

Affirmative	Negative	Interrogative
I could	I couldn't	Could I?
You could	You couldn't	Could you?
He could	He couldn't	Could he?
She could	She couldn't	Could she?
It could	It couldn't	Could it?
We could	We couldn't	Could we?
You could	You couldn't	Could you?
They could	They couldn't	Could they?

Summary of Tenses

Present Simple

Affirmative	Negative
I talk	I don't talk
You talk	You don't talk
He talks	He doesn't talk etc.
She talks	
It talks	**Interrogative**
We talk	Do I talk?
You talk	Do you talk?
They talk	Does he talk? etc.

Present Continuous

Affirmative	Negative
I am talking	I'm not talking
You are talking	You aren't talking
He is talking	He isn't talking etc.
She is talking	
It is talking	**Interrogative**
We are talking	Am I talking?
You are talking	Are you talking?
They are talking	Is he talking? etc.

Future Simple

Affirmative	Negative
I will talk	I won't talk
You will talk	You won't talk
He will talk	He won't talk etc.
She will talk	
It will talk	**Interrogative**
We will talk	Shall I talk?
You will talk	Will you talk?
They will talk	Will he talk? etc.

Present Perfect

Affirmative	Negative
I have talked	I haven't talked
You have talked	You haven't talked
He has talked	He hasn't talked etc.
She has talked	
It has talked	**Interrogative**
We have talked	Have I talked?
You have talked	Have you talked?
They have talked	Has he talked? etc.

Present Perfect Continuous

Affirmative	Negative
I have been talking	I haven't been talking
You have been talking	You haven't been talking
He has been talking	He hasn't been talking etc.
She has been talking	
It has been talking	**Interrogative**
We have been talking	Have I been talking?
You have been talking	Have you been talking?
They have been talking	Has he been talking? etc.

Past Simple

Affirmative	Negative
I talked	I didn't talk
You talked	You didn't talk
He talked	He didn't talk etc.
She talked	
It talked	**Interrogative**
We talked	Did I talk?
You talked	Did you talk?
They talked	Did he talk? etc.

Past Continuous

Affirmative	Negative
I was talking	I wasn't talking
You were talking	You weren't talking
He was talking	He wasn't talking etc.
She was talking	
It was talking	**Interrogative**
We were talking	Was I talking?
You were talking	Were you talking?
They were talking	Was he talking? etc.

Past Perfect

Affirmative	Negative
I had talked	I hadn't talked
You had talked	You hadn't talked
He had talked	He hadn't talked etc.
She had talked	
It had talked	**Interrogative**
We had talked	Had I talked?
You had talked	Had you talked?
They had talked	Had he talked? etc.

Past Perfect Continuous

Affirmative	Negative
I had been talking	I hadn't been talking
You had been talking	You hadn't been talking
He had been talking	He hadn't been talking etc.
She had been talking	
It had been talking	**Interrogative**
We had been talking	Had I been talking?
You had been talking	Had you been talking?
They had been talking	Had he been talking? etc.

Irregular Verbs

Infinitive	Past	Past Participle	Infinitive	Past	Past Participle
be	was	been	lie	lay	lain
bear	bore	born(e)	light	lit	lit
beat	beat	beaten	lose	lost	lost
become	became	become	make	made	made
begin	began	begun	mean	meant	meant
bite	bit	bitten	meet	met	met
blow	blew	blown	pay	paid	paid
break	broke	broken	put	put	put
bring	brought	brought	read	read	read
build	built	built	ride	rode	ridden
burn	burnt	burnt	ring	rang	rung
burst	burst	burst	rise	rose	risen
buy	bought	bought	run	ran	run
can	could	(been able to)	say	said	said
catch	caught	caught	see	saw	seen
choose	chose	chosen	seek	sought	sought
come	came	come	sell	sold	sold
cost	cost	cost	send	sent	sent
cut	cut	cut	set	set	set
deal	dealt	dealt	sew	sewed	sewn
dig	dug	dug	shake	shook	shaken
do	did	done	shine	shone	shone
draw	drew	drawn	shoot	shot	shot
dream	dreamt	dreamt	show	showed	shown
drink	drank	drunk	shut	shut	shut
drive	drove	driven	sing	sang	sung
eat	ate	eaten	sit	sat	sat
fall	fell	fallen	sleep	slept	slept
feed	fed	fed	smell	smelt	smelt
feel	felt	felt	speak	spoke	spoken
fight	fought	fought	spell	spelt	spelt
find	found	found	spend	spent	spent
fly	flew	flown	spill	spilt	spilt
forbid	forbade	forbidden	split	split	split
forget	forgot	forgotten	spoil	spoilt	spoilt
forgive	forgave	forgiven	spread	spread	spread
freeze	froze	frozen	spring	sprang	sprung
get	got	got	stand	stood	stood
give	gave	given	steal	stole	stolen
go	went	gone	stick	stuck	stuck
grow	grew	grown	sting	stung	stung
hang	hung	hung	strike	struck	struck
have	had	had	swear	swore	sworn
hear	heard	heard	sweep	swept	swept
hide	hid	hidden	swim	swam	swum
hit	hit	hit	take	took	taken
hold	held	held	teach	taught	taught
hurt	hurt	hurt	tear	tore	torn
keep	kept	kept	tell	told	told
know	knew	known	think	thought	thought
lay	laid	laid	throw	threw	thrown
lead	led	led	understand	understood	understood
learn	learnt	learnt	wake	woke	woken
leave	left	left	wear	wore	worn
lend	lent	lent	win	won	won
let	let	let	write	wrote	written

144

Pre-Test 1

A. Put the verbs in brackets into Present Simple or Present Continuous.

Dear Clare,

I (1) .... (love) Manchester! I (2) .... (work) for a translating company in the city centre at the moment. I really (3) .... (enjoy) the work and the people here (4) .... (be) very friendly. We (5) .... (go) to the cinema once a week and tomorrow Bill (6) .... (have) a party.
I (7) .... (stay) with my aunt and uncle until I (8) .... (find) a flat of my own. They (9) .... (help) me a lot, but it (10) .... (be) still hard work trying to find somewhere to stay.

Write soon,
Jo

B. Put the verbs in brackets into Present Simple or Present Continuous.

Dear Isabel,

Oxford (11) .... (be) beautiful! I (12) .... (study) German and Russian at the University here. I (13) .... (find) the work very interesting, but difficult! The other people on the course (14) .... (feel) the same way! We all (15) .... (meet) up once a week to discuss the lectures and compositions and tomorrow, we (16) .... (go) to London for an important lecture.
I (17) .... (stay) in student accommodation for the moment, but some of us (18) .... (look for) a house to share. The food in the hall (19) .... (be) disgusting, so we usually (20) .... (have) lunch in a small restaurant near the University.

Write soon,
Bill

C. Fill in: "has - have been in / to", "has - have gone to".

21. Belinda .... the dentist. She'll be back at 6.00 pm.
22. Nigel and Nancy .... Mexico on honeymoon. I saw them yesterday.
23. They .... the office for hours! What are they doing?
24. The Browns .... Vienna on holiday. I hope they'll have a good time.

D. Fill in: "has - have been in / to", "has - have gone to".

25. Sarah .... Austria for six weeks. I don't think she is ever coming back.
26. I'm sorry, Mrs Bowes is not here. She .... Munich on business.
27. They .... Russia before. Haven't you seen their photographs?
28. I .... the doctor's and he has given me some pills.

Round-up 4 — Pre-Test 1

E. Put the verbs in brackets into Present Perfect or Past Simple.

Tina: What (29) .... (you/do) last weekend?
Jane: I (30) .... (spend) the weekend in Bristol and I (31) .... (just/return).
Tina: I (32) .... (never/be) to Bristol. What's it like?
Jane: Friends of mine (33) .... (live) there for five years so they know some interesting, fun places.
Tina: (34) .... (you/enjoy) yourself?
Jane: Yes. It (35) .... (be) great! I (36) .... (not/have) such a good time for ages.
Tina: That's good. (37) .... (you/decide) what you're doing this weekend?
Jane: I (38) .... (already/invite) my friends from Bristol to stay with me for the weekend.

F. Put the verbs in brackets into Present Perfect or Past Simple.

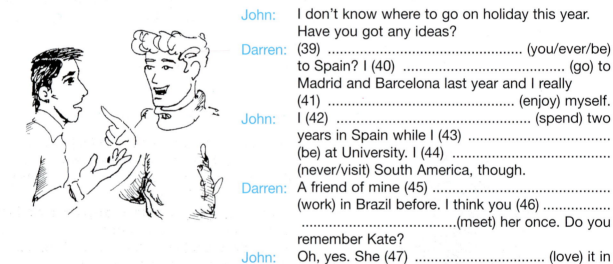

John: I don't know where to go on holiday this year. Have you got any ideas?
Darren: (39) .... (you/ever/be) to Spain? I (40) .... (go) to Madrid and Barcelona last year and I really (41) .... (enjoy) myself.
John: I (42) .... (spend) two years in Spain while I (43) .... (be) at University. I (44) .... (never/visit) South America, though.
Darren: A friend of mine (45) .... (work) in Brazil before. I think you (46) .... (meet) her once. Do you remember Kate?
John: Oh, yes. She (47) .... (love) it in Brazil. Maybe I'll talk to her about it.

G. Rewrite the sentences in the correct order.

48. plays / piano / she / the / beautifully ....
49. small / she / a / French / brown / table / has ....
50. gave / me / he / beautiful / ring / a / gold ....
51. never / arrives / he / before / at work / 10 o'clock ....
52. wore / a pair of / shoes / plastic / black / old / she ....

Round-up 4 — Pre-Test 1

H. Rewrite the sentences in the correct order.

53. always / writes / neatly / she ....
54. owns / she / lovely / a / house / old ....
55. I / at 6 o'clock / every day / swimming / go ....
56. by taxi / to work / comes / usually / he ....
57. never / to the beach / in winter / go / we ....

I. Fill in: "than", "of" or "in" and the correct comparative or superlative form.

Bob: Hi, Jane. I saw (58) .... (good) film ever last night.
Jane: What was it called?
Bob: "Wild Wild West". It was (59) .... (exciting) .... "Tomorrow Never Comes" and it was (60) .... (funny) .... any other comedy I've seen this year. Will Smith is (61) .... (handsome) man .... the world! He is a much (62) .... (good) actor .... Pierce Brosnan. And the machine! It is (63) .... (amazing) machine .... the world! Have you seen the film?
Jane: Yes, but I have seen much (64) .... (amusing) films. I didn't think it was that good. "Notting Hill" is (65) .... (funny) film .... them all.

J. Fill in: "than", "of" or "in" and the correct comparative or superlative form.

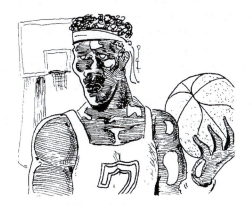

Martin Hamble is a member of (66) .... (famous) basketball team .... the world. He is (67) .... (tall) and (68) .... (young) player .... the team. Martin is a very good player, but his friend, Jim, is (69) .... (good) ....he is. Matthew Bodine is (70) .... (old) .... Jim and Martin and he's also (71) .... (fast) .... both of them. He is (72)............... .... (exciting) player to watch and also (73) .... (popular) member .... the team.

K. Fill in: "will", "shall" or "be going to".

74. What .... we do tonight?
75. She .... probably pass her exams.
76. I've worked hard this summer. Now I .... have a holiday.
77. Be careful! Otherwise you .... hurt yourself.
78. Look! Tim .... win! He's much faster than the other runners.

Round-up 4 — Pre-Test 1

L. Fill in: "will", "shall" or "be going to".

79. I'm afraid I .... not be able to come to your party.
80. .... we go to Spain for our holiday this year?
81. She .... travel around the world. She's leaving on Friday.
82. He .... buy a better car if he gets the job.
83. I .... start my university course in September.

M. Choose the correct item.

84. He's .... person I've ever met.
    A) the friendlier   B) friendly
    C) the friendliest

85. She .... a letter at the moment.
    A) is writing   B) writes   C) has written

86. They haven't seen each other .... they left school.
    A) after   B) since   C) for

87. I think Holland .... win the World Cup.
    A) is going to   B) will   C) shall

88. My mother .... in a hospital. She's a nurse.
    A) works   B) is working   C) has worked

89. My bag is .... than hers.
    A) the heavier   B) heavier
    C) heaviest

90. Mike is .... lazier than Dave.
    A) very   B) less   C) much

91. Have you seen "The Phantom Menace" .... ?
    A) yet   B) already   C) just

92. He .... in Italy for two years.
    A) lives   B) is living   C) has lived

93. He .... his leg, so he can't play football today.
    A) has broken   B) breaks   C) is breaking

94. Jim .... a bath at the moment.
    A) is having   B) has   C) has had

95. This is .... time I've spent away from home.
    A) longer   B) long   C) the longest

96. He is .... nicer than his brother.
    A) more   B) less   C) much

97. I haven't been to Portsmouth .... three years.
    A) since   B) for   C) after

98. I .... the cooking if you do the washing-up.
    A) do   B) will do   C) did

99. I've .... tidied my bedroom.
    A) already   B) yet   C) since

100. Where are the .... coats?
    A) childrens'   B) children'
    C) children

148

Pre-Test 2

A. Put the verbs in brackets into Present Perfect Simple or Present Perfect Continuous.

1. Don't walk in there! I .... (just/clean) the floor.
2. Jane's hungry. She .... (not/eat) anything for six hours.
3. She is tired. She .... (study) for four hours.
4. I don't want to see that film again. I .... (see) it twice already.
5. Sandy .... (teach) English for ten years.
6. Chris .... (not/do) the washing-up yet.
7. He .... (work) all morning.
8. They .... (play) in the garden for two hours.

B. Put the verbs in brackets into Past Simple or Past Continuous.

I (9) .... (watch) TV last night when I (10) .... (hear) a strange noise outside my window. I (11) .... (be) frightened, but I decided to investigate. As I (12) .... (walk) towards the window the curtains (13) .... (start) to move. I (14) .... (scream) loudly and my mother (15) .... (run) in. Then I (16) .... (realise) that the noise was my cat trying to climb in through the window.

C. Put the verbs in brackets into Past Simple or Past Continuous.

My friend (17) .... (walk) home from school last week when she (18) .... (hear) a loud bang. Some men (19) .... (rob) a bank. She quickly (20) .... (run) to a telephone and (21) .... (call) the police. The police (22) .... (arrive) and (23) .... (arrest) the men. The next day the bank manager (24) .... (give) my friend some flowers and her picture was in the local newspaper.

D. Fill in: "used to" or "didn't use to".

When I was a little girl, I (25) .... be very unhappy, but I'm not now. I (26) .... have any friends and I (27) .... cry a lot. I (28) .... talk to anybody, but I do now.

Round-up 4   Pre-Test 2

E. Fill in: "used to" or "didn't use to".

When James was a little boy he (29) .... play with his toy cars quite often. He (30) .... drive a real car, but he (31) .... ride his bicycle every day. He (32) .... like reading books, but he does now.

F. Fill in the correct pronouns or possessive adjectives.

My mother was cooking when she cut (33) .... with a knife. "Come quickly", she said to (34) .... "I've cut (35) ...." I ran to the kitchen to help (36) .... When I saw her I laughed and said "Mum, you haven't cut (37) .... You have just spilt tomato sauce on (38) .... hand."

G. Fill in the correct pronouns or possessive adjectives.

My aunt and uncle live in Paris. (39) .... house is very big. They do most of the work (40) .... My aunt works in the garden and (41) .... friends say it is the best garden in the world! My uncle does most of the painting (42) .... , but (43) .... friend, Mr Brown often helps (44) ....

H. Fill in: "any", "anything", "no", "nothing", "some", "somebody", "somewhere" or "nowhere".

45. I heard a noise, but my father couldn't hear ....
46. Would you like .... chocolate?
47. .... left a book in the classroom. It's on the floor.
48. I'm afraid there is .... coffee left. Can you go and buy some?
49. She doesn't know .... about history.
50. .... has stolen my bag.
51. Are there .... cakes left? I'm hungry.
52. I want to go .... interesting on holiday.
53. I can't find my glasses; they are ....
54. I'm thirsty; I've had .... to drink all day.

I. Put the verbs in brackets into Past Perfect Simple or Past Perfect Continuous.

55. I was tired because I .... (work) too hard all day.
56. When I got to the station, the last train .... (already/leave).
57. Ben .... (live) in Rome for two years before he moved to Paris.
58. Sally .... (eat) so much chocolate that she felt sick.
59. My hand was hurting because I .... (write) all day.
60. I got wet because I .... (forget) to take my umbrella.
61. He was pleased because he .... (pass) his exam.
62. I .... (study) for three days before I took my test.

Round-up 4 — Pre-Test 2

J. Choose the correct item.

63. John .... down the road when he fell.
    A) walked B) was walking C) had walked

64. My friend and I had a lovely holiday. .... of us wanted to go home.
    A) Neither B) All C) None

65. Jane is the .... person I know.
    A) cleverest B) cleverer C) more clever

66. George and Tom are friends. .... of them work in a bank.
    A) All B) None C) Both

67. My dog is .... than my friend's dog.
    A) bigger B) the biggest C) big

68. I have never .... Paris.
    A) gone to B) been to C) been in

69. .... of my family like football.
    A) Neither B) Both C) None

70. There is .... in the cupboards. We have to go to the supermarket.
    A) nothing B) everything C) anything

71. Jane .... the hairdresser's; she'll be back at 3 o'clock.
    A) has been to B) has gone to C) has been in

72. I have two cousins. .... of them are good students.
    A) Both B) Neither C) None

73. I have a lot of friends in the USA, but .... of them have visited me in Portugal.
    A) none B) neither C) both

74. It was the .... coat she had ever bought.
    A) most expensive B) more expensive C) expensive

75. The weather is .... today than it was yesterday.
    A) better B) good C) best

76. .... I answer the phone?
    A) Shall B) Do C) Will

77. .... breakfast every morning?
    A) Are you having B) Do you have C) Had you had

78. John .... football, when he broke his arm.
    A) play B) played C) was playing

79. Tom sings ....
    A) beautiful B) good C) beautifully

80. I have two sisters. ...... of them live in Athens.
    A) None B) Neither C) All

81. John is tired because he .... all day long.
    A) studied B) has been studying C) had studied

82. Simon .... France for his holiday. He's been there for 3 weeks.
    A) has gone in B) has been to C) has gone to

83. Dave and Ben can play the guitar but .... of them can sing.
    A) neither B) all C) none

84. .... I cook dinner tonight?
    A) Will B) Shall C) Do

K. Put the verbs in brackets into the correct tense.

My uncle Quentin (85) .... (travel) to Rome frequently.
He (86) .... (already/go) there twice this month.
He (87) .... (fall) in love with a beautiful Italian woman two years ago and he
(88) .... (visit) her ever since. I think he
(89) .... (marry) her soon.

151

Round-up 4 — Pre-Test 2

L. Put the verbs in brackets into the correct tense.

The Queen (90) .... (have) a garden party at Buckingham Palace every year. Last year she (91) .... (invite) a friend of mine. He (92) .... (borrow) some money from me to buy a new outfit and he (93) .... (still/try) to pay it all back. I think I (94) .... (write) to Her Majesty and ask her not to invite him again!

M. Put the verbs in brackets into the correct tense.

95. He felt tired. He .... (drive) all day.

96. Oh no! I .... (lose) my wallet!

97. Ann is exhausted. She .... (type) letters all morning.

98. He was wet. He .... (walk) in the rain.

99. Sally's eyes are sore. She .... (read) for hours.

100. He was happy because he .... (win) the race.

Pre-Test 3

A. Fill in: "don't have to", "may", "can't", "should", "shall" or "must".

1. You .... put your litter in the bin.

2. You .... eat your lunch now. Eat it later.

3. He's sleeping on the bench. He .... be rich.

4. Excuse me. .... I help you with your suitcase?

5. .... I use your phone, please?

6. You .... obey the school rules.

B. Fill in: "shall", "mustn't", "should", "can't", "don't have to" or "may".

7. You .... buy a new car.

8. .... we go to the cinema?

9. You .... talk during an exam.

10. .... I sit there?

11. She .... be his grandmother; she looks very young.

12. You .... take an umbrella with you. The weather's fine!

Round-up 4 — Pre-Test 3

C. Complete the dialogue.

G: Hello Sam.
S: Hello Gary. That's my new car there.
G: (13) .... ?
S: My car is the red one.
G: (14) .... ?
S: I bought it last week.
G: (15) .... ?
S: Yes, it goes very fast.
G: (16) .... ?
S: My cousin sold it to me.
G: (17) .... ?
S: Yes, I drive it to work every day.
G: (18) .... ?
S: Yes, of course you can borrow it.

D. Complete the dialogue.

J: Hello Mike. (19) .... ?
M: I'm going shopping.
J: (20) .... ?
M: I'm going with my friend, Anne.
J: (21) .... ?
M: We're going to buy some records for our party.
J: (22) .... ?
M: Yes, I like pop music very much.
J: (23) .... ?
M: Yes, I have bought Michael Jackson's last record.
J: (24) .... ?
M: I bought it when it was number 1 in the charts.

E. Add question tags and short answers.

25. I've met you before, ... ? Yes, ...
26. I'm in the same class as you, ... ? Yes, ...
27. Your brother is our teacher, ... ? Yes, ...
28. He works hard, ... ? No, ...
29. You know about the bank robbery, ... ? No, ...
30. You've read the newspaper, ... ? No, ...
31. He lives next door, ... ? Yes, ...
32. She didn't pass her driving test last week, ... ? No, ...

F. Turn from Active into Passive.

(33) A farmer dug up a very old statue last week. (34) Somebody had buried it thousands of years ago. (35) The farmer took the statue to a museum. (36) Experts are repairing it. (37) The museum will put the statue on display. (38) The museum has given a reward to the farmer.

....
....
....
....
....
....

G. Turn from Active into Passive.

(39) Professor Golding found some jewellery in the rubbish. (40) Someone had thrown it out. (41) The Professor took it to the police. (42) The police are searching for the owner. (43) They have asked people lots of questions so far. (44) They will keep the jewellery in a safe place.

....
....
....
....
....

Round-up 4 Pre-Test 3

H. Put the verbs in brackets into the correct form (infinitive or gerund).

I've always wanted (45) .... (go) to China and last year my dream came true. I love (46) .... (travel). The travel agent suggested (47) .... (visit) the Great Wall first. After (48) .... (see) Beijing, we flew to Canton because it's too far (49) .... (go) by train. I enjoyed (50) .... (fly) over the rice-fields and villages.

I. Put the verbs in brackets into the correct form (infinitive or gerund).

I have a penfriend in Canada. I really like (51) .... (meet) new people so I started (52) .... (write) letters four years ago. At the moment, I'm busy (53) .... (arrange) a trip to Canada. I want (54) .... (meet) my penfriend, Alan. I hope (55) .... (go) sightseeing and I'm looking forward to (56) .... (stay) with Alan and his family.

J. Use the man's thoughts to write conditionals.

57. I didn't pay attention. I crashed the car.
58. I haven't got much money. I won't be able to pay for repairs.
59. I borrowed my friend's car. I had an accident.
60. I'll drive more carefully in future. I won't have another accident.
61. I am not an experienced driver. I'm not a very good driver.
62. I didn't see the tree. I crashed into it.

57. ....
58. ....
59. ....
60. ....
61. ....
62. ....

K. Use the boy's thoughts to write conditionals.

63. I don't have a map. I can't find the way.
64. The weather is bad. I feel cold and wet.
65. There's no telephone. I can't call my mum to pick me up.
66. I missed the bus. I walked in the rain.
67. A car will go past. I will ask for a lift.
68. It's so dark. I feel scared.

63. ....
64. ....
65. ....
66. ....
67. ....
68. ....

Round-up 4 — Pre-Test 3

L. Put the verbs in brackets into the correct tense.

I (69) .... (drive) in the countryside last week when I (70) .... (see) something strange. A horse (71) .... (escape) from a field and three people (72) .... (run) after it. The odd thing (73) .... (be) that the horse (74) .... (wear) a clown's costume, just like a horse in the circus! I (75) .... (not/think) I (76) .... (ever/see) anything so funny before.

M. Put the verbs in brackets into the correct tense.

Last week Anne (77) .... (start) a new job in a hospital. She (78) .... (work) there for six days now and she really (79) .... (like) the job. She (80) .... (find) the first two days difficult because she (81) .... (not / do) this type of job before. At the moment she (82) .... (try) to learn a lot of new things about the job. She (83) .... (hope) she (84) .... (learn) everything quickly.

N. Choose the correct item.

85. I finished the project but my friends didn't finish ....
    A) them   B) theirs   C) their

86. He's tired. He .... since 9 o'clock.
    A) has been studying   B) studies
    C) has studied

87. I want to go .... hot on holiday. I think I'll go to Spain.
    A) nowhere   B) anywhere
    C) somewhere

88. She's at the bus-stop. She .... catch a bus.
    A) is going to   B) will   C) shall

89. I hate driving my .... car.
    A) fathers   B) father's   C) fathers'

90. I wish the students were ....
    A) quietly   B) quiet   C) quietest

91. When my sister passed her exams, she was pleased with ....
    A) her   B) herself   C) her's

92. If you want a cup of tea, make it ....
    A) yourself   B) yours   C) you

93. I think Germany .... win the football match.
    A) is going to   B) shall   C) will

94. I have four children, but .... of them are tall.
    A) none   B) neither   C) both

95. She is very busy today. She .... letters all morning.
    A) has been typing   B) had typed
    C) had been typing

96. Lisa and Frank have no money. .... of them is rich.
    A) None   B) Neither   C) All

97. .... you like to order now, sir?
    A) Will   B) Shall   C) Would

98. She is the .... swimmer in the team.
    A) slowest   B) slower   C) slowly

99. It's taken me a long time to clear away the .... toys.
    A) children   B) childrens'   C) children's

100. This is Jim's bicycle. It's ....
    A) his   B) hers   C) himself

Pre-Test 4

A. Fill in: "why", "where", "who", "whose", "which" or "when".

Dear Sally and Bob,

We're having a wonderful time here in Spain. (1) .... we arrived it was very hot but now it's cooler. The hotel (2) .... we are staying is lovely, and the staff (3) .... work here are very helpful. The beach, (4) .... is right in front of our hotel, is beautiful and the water is so warm! We sunbathe everyday so if we have a good tan, you'll know the reason (5) .... ! We've met a nice man (6) .... father owns a yacht and tomorrow he's taking us sailing!
That's all our news. See you soon.

Love,
John and Mary

B. Fill in: "who", "whose", "which", "when", "why" or "where".

Dear Terry and June,

Sorry we haven't written for so long but we've been very busy decorating our new house. The reason (7) .... it needs so much work is that it is over two hundred years old. The village (8) .... we live now is very old and pretty and the house (9) .... is next door is over 300 years old. The couple (10) .... live next door are very sweet, but the man (11) .... house is behind ours isn't. In the evenings, (12) .... I sit in the garden, he lights a fire in his garden and all the smoke blows into my face! Anyway, we're happy in our new home and looking forward to you visiting us.

Love,
Bob and Mary

C. Fill in: "a", "an" or "the" where necessary.

Last summer I visited (13) .... New York. I stayed at (14) .... Hilton Hotel. I could see (15) .... Statue of Liberty from my window. One day I crossed (16) .... Hudson River and had lunch in (17) .... expensive restaurant.

D. Fill in: "a", "an" or "the" where necessary.

Last month we went to (18) .... England. We had (19) .... wonderful holiday. On our first day we went to (20) .... Tower of London. It was fantastic! Then we went on (21) .... interesting tour of London. London is (22) .... most fascinating city I've ever been to.

E. Turn from Active into Passive.

(23) Somebody stole Jane's bicycle yesterday. (24) He took it from outside the super-market. (25) Somebody told her that a boy had stolen it. (26) Fortunately a policeman stopped him. (27) He returned the bicycle to her.

....
....
....
....
....

Round-up 4 — Pre-Test 4

F. Write what the people said using Reported Speech.

28. The shopkeeper told his assistant ....
29. The shop assistant said ....
30. Mrs Boyle asked them ....
31. Mrs Grady asked them ....
32. Mrs Kent told Tom ....
33. Tom asked Mrs Kent ....
34. Alison said ....
35. Mr Smith said ....

G. Write what the people said using Reported Speech.

36. The photographer told everyone ....
37. The bride said ....
38. The groom asked the bride ....
39. Mrs Bowl asked the photographer ....
40. Mr Bowl said ....
41. Mr Lee asked ....
42. Granny said ....
43. Grandad said ....

Round-up 4   Pre-Test 4

H. Write what the people wish.

44. ....

Bob can't go skiing.

45. ....

David can't go to the dance.

46. ....

Sally's missed the bus.

47. ....

He didn't see the cat. He tripped over it.

48. ....

She bought these shoes. They hurt her feet.

49. ....

He wants to be good at football.

50. ....

The children won't stop talking. The teacher has a headache.

51. ....

His grandmother always shouts at him. He doesn't want her to do it.

52. ....

Charles doesn't want to see the dentist, but he has to.

53. ....

Mandy's suitcase is very heavy. She can't lift it.

54. ....

Nick ate a whole cake and now he feels sick.

55. ....

Bob lost his car keys and now he can't drive his car.

Round-up 4 — Pre-Test 4

I. Fill in the blanks using the appropriate tense

Tom likes going to evening classes. At the moment he (56) .... (learn) how to repair cars. Sometimes the teacher, Mr Jones, (57) .... (let) the students work on his car, but last night something (58) .... (happen) which made him change his mind. Mr Jones (59) .... (teach) for 15 years and he (60) .... (always/trust) his students to do things correctly, but last night while Tom (61) .... (work) on Mr Jones' car, somebody (62) .... (call) Mr Jones to the phone. He (63) .... (only/be) away for a few minutes when he heard shouting from the workshop. He ran back and saw that his car (64) .... (burn)! Tom (65) .... (drop) a lighted match into the engine and set it on fire.

J. Fill in the blanks using the appropriate tense.

Sally (66) .... (live) in Madrid. She (67) .... (live) there for six years now. She (68) .... (move) there when she was twenty-five years old. After she (69) .... (leave) university in 1988 she decided to leave England and go to work abroad. One day while she (70) .... (read) a newspaper, she saw a job advertised for a teacher in Madrid. She (71) .... (decide) to apply and she got the job. At the moment she (72) .... (work) at a primary school. She (73) .... (teach) a lot of students so far. Today she (74) .... (teach) her favourite class so she (75) .... (really/enjoy) the lesson.

K. Turn from Active into Passive.

(76) A fire burnt down Forrest Castle last night. (77) Some people were holding a party in the main hall. (78) A cigarette started the fire. (79) Fortunately they had removed most of the valuable paintings the day before. (80) The Queen will visit the castle tomorrow.

....
....
....
....
....

L. Use the woman's thoughts to write conditionals.

81. I don't know anyone at this party. I'm not enjoying it.

82. There is no telephone. I can't call a taxi.

83. I didn't have any money. I didn't buy a new dress for the party.

84. I'll get to bed late. I'll be tired all day tomorrow.

81. ....
82. ....
83. ....
84. ....

Round-up 4 — Pre-Test 4

M. Fill in: "on", "in", "in front of", "opposite", "through" or "under".

This is Sarah's room. There is a picture (85) .... the wall. There's a desk (86) .... the picture and a chair (87) .... the desk. (88) .... the window there is a chest of drawers where Sally keeps her clothes. Her mother is coming in (89) .... the door. Sally's clothes are not (90) .... the drawers, they are on the floor! Her mother is very angry.

N. Fill in: "through", "next to", "behind", "in", "on" or "beside".

This is Susan's kitchen. She is standing (91) .... the cooker because she is cooking something. There are eggs and bacon (92) .... the frying pan. There is a clock (93) .... the wall. (94) .... the clock there is a shelf with some cookery books on it. Susan's cat is coming in (95) .... the window. Max, Susan's dog, is standing (96) .... the chair, waiting for his lunch.

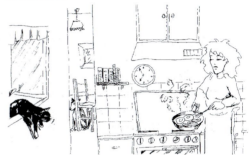

O. Choose the correct item.

97. You .... finish that work today, you can do it tomorrow.
    A) can't   B) may   C) needn't

98. Easter is .... May this year.
    A) in   B) on   C) at

99. Tom .... be rich. He always wears old clothes.
    A) might   B) can't   C) should

100. If you finish early, I ... you to the theatre.
    A) take   B) will take   C) would take

101. I have two brothers. They are .... tall.
    A) all   B) neither   C) both

102. Would you mind .... the cat out?
    A) letting   B) to let   C) let

103. This is my .... bike.
    A) mothers   B) mothers'   C) mother's

104. They have been driving ..... four hours.
    A) since   B) for   C) ago

105. My parents have been married .... twenty five years.
    A) for   B) ago   C) since

106. If you had looked carefully, you .... the banana skin.
    A) would see   B) saw   C) would have seen

107. I cut .... with a knife this morning.
    A) mine   B) my   C) myself

108. Would you like .... my holiday photographs?
    A) seeing   B) to see   C) see

109. She has been in Rome .... 1989.
    A) since   B) while   C) for

110. I .... buy a pair of new shoes.
    A) must   B) need   C) ought

111. I can't see my bicycle ....
    A) nowhere   B) anywhere   C) somewhere

112. He comes from Egypt, ... ?
    A) does he   B) isn't he   C) doesn't he

113. I didn't tell .... about it.
    A) somebody   B) nobody   C) anybody

114. I .... buy a new coat if I had enough money.
    A) would   B) am   C) will

Round-up 4 — Pre-Test 4

115. What would you do if you .... a million pounds?
A) win   B) won   C) will win

116. .... is wearing my hat?
A) Who   B) What   C) Why

117. It .... be raining outside – I can see people with umbrellas.
A) must   B) can   C) need

118. The plane leaves .... 9 o'clock tomorrow.
A) at   B) on   C) in

119. I think I .... go to my parents tonight.
A) will   B) am going to   C) would

120. I'm very pleased .... you again!
A) see   B) seeing   C) to see

121. .... Simon and Richard like Mary.
A) All   B) Both   C) Neither

122. He's ill. He hasn't been to school .... Tuesday.
A) ago   B) since   C) for

123. .... has stolen my purse!
A) Someone   B) No   C) Anyone

124. .... did you get home so late?
A) When   B) Why   C) Who

125. I think it .... be sunny tomorrow.
A) would   B) will   C) is

126. If we had arrived on time, we ... the film.
A) will see   B) would see   C) would have seen

127. They met at a party a year ....
A) since   B) for   C) ago

128. We .... go shopping today if you don't want to.
A) needn't   B) can't   C) may

129. I'm hungry but there's .... in the fridge for me to eat!
A) nothing   B) something   C) anything

130. That is my .... car.
A) grandfathers   B) grandfather's   C) grandfathers'

131. She's known me .... a long time.
A) for   B) since   C) ago

132. I'll give it to him if he ....
A) will come   B) comes   C) had come

133. There's no point .... her. She never helps anyone.
A) ask   B) to ask   C) asking

134. You drive a Mercedes, ... ?
A) don't you   B) didn't you   C) do you

135. Look at the cat! It's cleaning ....!
A) it   B) its   C) itself

136. If I knew his address, I .... to him.
A) write   B) will write   C) would write

P. Use the woman's thoughts to write conditionals.

137. I didn't get up early. I was late.
138. I don't speak French. I can't take the job.
139. I felt nervous. I started crying.
140. I'll apply for another job. I won't make the same mistakes.

137. ....
138. ....
139. ....
140. ....

Wordlist

A
ability
above
abroad
absence
accidentally
according to
accordingly
Accounting
accusative
accuse
across
act
Active Voice
activity
add
address
adjective
admit
adverb
advertisement
advice
advise
affirmative
afford
afterwards
against
age
agent
ago
agreement
alarm clock
alike
alive
allow
alone
along
Alps
already
alright
always
amazing
ambulance
among
ancient
anger
angrily
ankle
annoy
annoyance
annoyed
answer the door
any more
apologise
apology
appear
application
apply for
appointment
appropriate
area
argument
armed
arrange
arrangement
arrest
artist
as if
as long as
aspirin
at
at least
at once
at present
at sea
at the moment
athletic
attic
attract
attraction
auxiliary verb
available
average
avoid
awful
axe

B
babysit
background
bake
baker's
band
bank
bark
barn
be away
be held
be held up
be situated
be used to
bear
beard
beat
beauty products
beg
behave
below
beside
between
bike
bill
bin
blame
blank
blender
blow up
board
boat trip
bonnet
bored
boss
both
bottom
bowl
brainwash
branch
break down
break into
bride
bridge
brilliant
brochure
broom
brush
builder
bunch
burglar
burglary
burial
bury
bus-stop
butcher's
by

C
C.V.
cage
calendar
campsite
candle
capital
carelessly
carols
carpet
carry out
case
cashier's desk
catch up on
cave
celebrate
central
central heating
charge with
charity
chase
cheetah
chef
chemist's
cheque
chew
choice
chop
churchyard
city
clause
clerk
cliff
coach
coin
collect
column
comfortable
command
comment
company
comparative
competition
complain
completely
compound
conditionals
confess
confirmation
congratulations
conjunction
consider
consonant
contact
contact lenses
contain
contest
context
convinced
Council
countable
countryside
courage
course
cousin
crash into
crew
criticism
cross
crossword
crutches
crystal
curly
customer
customs officer
cycle

D
daily
dance hall
dangerous
darling
deaf
deck
declare
degree
delicious
deliver
deny
department store
departure gate
depressed
description
desert
design
designer
desperate
dessert
destination
destroy
detail
diary
dictionary
difference
dinosaur
direct
Direct Speech
direct to
direction
director
disappear
disaster
discuss
dislike
disturb
divide
do the shopping
do up
dog-like
double
down
driving licence
drown
dry
dry-clean
duration
Dutch
Duty Free shop

E
easily
economical
edge
effect
elderly
electricity bill
emergency
emphasis
emphatic
empty
enclose
encyclopaedia
end
enormous
environment
equipment
equivalent
escape
especially
essential
event
ever
every
everywhere
evidence
except (for)
exhibit
exhibition
exotic
expect
experience
expert
explain
explanation
explore
explorer
express
expression
external
extinguish
extra

163

Wordlist

F
fact
faithfully
fall down
fall over
fear
fierce
fight
find out
fingerprints
fire
fireworks
first aid kit
fix
fixed
flared
flat
flat tyre
flight
floppy
fluently
fly
follow
following
for
forbidden
forest
forever
formal
fox
French fries
frequency
friendliness
frightened
from ... to
fry
full
function
furniture
further
further/farther
fussy

G
gardening
gate
general
genie
gently
gerund
get away
ghost
giraffe
glad
glove
go off
god
good times
good-looking
goods
grid
grocer's
groom

grow up
guard
guest
gunshot
gym

H
habit
hairstyle
hammer
hamster
handle
harbour
hard of hearing
hard-working
hardly
head
headache
headline
healthy
heavy traffic
helpful
hesitate
hint
hire
homeless
hope
horror
housewife
housework
how long
how long ago
how many
how much
how often
however
huge
hunt
hurry
hut

I
identify
illegal
implication
improve
in front of
in the end
in time
in turn
in/inside
include
Indonesian
indoors
industry
infinitive
informal
information
inside
install
instead of
instruction
intelligent

intend
intention
interest
interrupt
interview
into
intonation
introduce
invent
irregular
irritation
it's no use
it's worth

J
jewellery
jewellery shop
jigsaw
jogging
join
journalist
jumper
jungle
just
just now

K
knit
knock

L
laboratory
ladder
lake
lamp post
last
laundry room
Law
lazily
leading role
leak
lean
leather
lecture
let
lie
lifeboat
lift
light fittings
lightning
limited
litter
local
lock
locksmith
lonely
long hours
look for
look forward to
lottery
lovely
luckily

luxurious

M
mail-order company
majority
make up
manner
market
marriage
material
mean
mechanic
Medicine
medicine
Mediterranean
megaphone
memories
mess
message
messenger boy
microphone
millionaire
mind
model
monthly
mop
mountain range
move
movement
murder

N
nasty
naughty
near
nearby
nearest
nearly
necessity
negative
neighbourhood
neither
never
next
next to
nightclothes
noisy
none
normal
normally
north-east
novel
now

O
obey
object
object to
obligation
obliged
obvious
occasion

off
offer
Office Management
often
old people's home
old-fashioned
Olympic Games
omit
on
on business
on foot
on the way
on time
on-the-spot decision
once
one-way
onto
opinion
opposite
opposition leader
oral
order
organise
origin
ouch
out of
out of breath
outskirts
over
oversleep
overtime
overweight
own

P
Pacific
painting
palm tree
paper
partner
Passive Voice
past
path
patiently
pavement
Peloponnesian war
penguin
penicillin
perform
permanent
permission
personal
pet shop
petrol consumption
Pharaoh
philosopher
phrase
physical
pick
picks up
pickpocket
pie
pillow
plan

Wordlist

planet
plant
playfully
pleasure
plumber
pocket money
poison
polite
politely
popular
position
positive
possess
possession
possessive
possessive case
possibility
post
pray
prayers
prediction
preposition
present
present sb with
pretend
previous
price
prize
produce
progress
prohibition
project
promise
pronoun
proper noun
properly
protest
prove
public
public money
puppy
purpose

Q
qualifications
quantity
question
queue
quotation marks

R
race
radio transmitter
raft
rain cats and dogs
rarely
reach
read out
real
realise
receive
recently
rectangular

refer
reflexive
regard as
regret
relationship
relative
remake
repair
repeated
replace
Reported Speech
represent
request
rescue
result
ridiculous
rise
risk
rob
romantic
roof
rough
round
route
rubbish
rude
run away
run out
run out of
rush into

S
safe
safety-deposit box
salesperson
saucepan
say so
scared
science institute
scout
sculptor
seagull
seaside
second-hand
secretarial post
seem
seldom
separately
serve
set
set off
several times
shape
share
shark
shopping centre
shorthand
shout at
shower
sign
simultaneous
since
situation
size

skeleton
sleepwalking
slippers
smart
snowball
snowman
snowstorm
so far
sofa
soldier
sometime
sometimes
soon
sore feet
sore throat
specific
speech situation
Sphinx
spill
sponge cake
sponsor
sports centre
staff
stain
stall
stand on end
state
statement
statue
stay
stay up
stimulus
sting
stomachache
stone
stone structure
straight
strangely
stressed
stroke
struck
subject
substance
suburb
suggest
suggestion
sunbed
sunburnt
sunny
sunshade
suntan
suntan oil
superlative
support
suppose
survivor
swallow
swear
sweep away
sword
symptom

T
tag
take a while

take care of
take off
talk
team
teenage
tell one from another
temper
temporary
then
there's no point (in)
threaten
through
throughout
tidy
tie somebody up
tight
timetable
tiny
tip
tobacco
tomb
tomorrow
tonight
tool
top
torch
towards
traffic jam
traffic warden
train
training
transfer
tray
treasure
treat
trip
trip over
trouble
turkey
turn down
twice
twins
twist
two-storey
type
typing speed

U
uncountable
under
unfulfilled
uniform
unique
United Kingdom
unknown
unless
unreal
unstated
until
untrue
unusual
up
upset
usually

V
valuables
variety
van
vegetable
vegetarian
versus
village
visible
vowel

W
waitress
wallet
warden
warn
warning
waste
wastepaper bin
watch out
water
wave
weather
wedding dress
welcome
well
wet
what
what time
what's the matter?
when
where
which
whisper
who
whom
whose
why
wide
widow
will
wipe
wire
witch
wonder
wooden
woods
woollen
wpm
  (words per minute)
wrap

Y
yesterday
yet
youth

Z
zoo-keeper